The Kingdom, The Power & The Glory

Manifesting the Kingdom of God

Anthony Reinglas

Xtreme Publishing House

The Kingdom, The Power &
The Glory

To the prophets of the Old Testament who foreshadowed the coming of the Kingdom; to the Apostles and Prophets of the New Testament who preached the Kingdom not in Word only, but in Power, and my Lord and Savior, The King of all kings, Jesus Christ who came to restore us unto His Kingdom.

CONTENTS

CONTENTS

Printed in the United States of America
ISBN 979-8-9861871-0-5 [Softcover]
     979-8-9861871-1-2 [eBook]
     979-8-9861871-2-9 [Audio Book]

Xtreme Publishing House
XtremePublishingHouse.com

Unless noted, all scriptures are taken from the King James Version

Foreword

(Do not move forward before reading this section!)

I know this statement sounds very familiar, and believe me when I say this...it is a statement of truth. Hear what the Lord Jesus told the religious ruler Nicodemus:

John 3:3
> *Jesus answered and said unto him, Verily, verily, I say unto thee, except a man be born again, he cannot see the Kingdom of God.*

Be aware that He only spoke of this once throughout the four Gospels. He stated that without this process, one can't even see the Kingdom. Now I looked up that word "see" and in the Greek it is Strong's 3708 / *Horaó* which means to perceive, comprehend or understand. So unless you are born again, Jesus is saying that you cannot even perceive or understand the Kingdom of God. So for this book to make sense to you, and for you to truly reap the rewards and benefits I will unlock, you must be born again; otherwise you are wasting your time and energy even reading it.

Keep in mind, that being **born again** is a step. It is an indispensable step; because Jesus goes on to say to Nicodemus in verse 5&6: "Very truly I tell you, no one can enter the kingdom of God unless they are born of water and the Spirit. Flesh gives birth to flesh, but the Spirit gives birth to spirit.

And then He takes it a step further and states that not only will you not understand or come to perceive the Kingdom, but we cannot get into the Kingdom of Heaven or have eternal life without our spirit being born again.

> [16] For God so loved the world that he gave his one and only Son, that whoever believes in him shall not perish but have eternal life. [17] For God did not send his Son into the world to condemn the world, but to save the world through him. [18] Whoever believes in him is not condemned, but whoever does not believe stands condemned already because they have not believed in the name of God's one and only Son.

Being born again is the first step in a process of a whole new life. It is a journey of learning to know, appreciate and experience our rights, privileges, and responsibilities as Kingdom Citizens. So what exactly does that mean and how do I become born again? I copied this from a Billy Graham website:

> Our first birth gave us physical life; the new birth gives us spiritual life and membership in God's family (John 1:13). To be born again is to have the Holy Spirit transform our hearts from indifference and hostility toward God to a love of God and a desire for righteousness and holiness. The only way one can come to God and experience what it means to be "born again" is through repentance of sin and faith in Jesus Christ; read John 14:6. The Bible clearly teaches in Ephesians 2:8-10, Titus 3:5, and Romans 10:13 that salvation is a gift; it cannot be earned in any way.
>
> To receive Jesus Christ as Savior and Lord means more than accepting Him as a fact of history, a teacher, or an example. It means more than giving mental assent to the fact that Jesus died on the cross for the sins of the world. It means that one turns from sin and with his or her whole heart trusts in Christ

as personal Savior and Lord. God makes that one a new person; see 2 Corinthians 5:17. The Bible says, "To all who received him, to those who believed in his name, he gave the right to become children of God" (John 1:12).

Are you ready to put your faith in Christ to be born again so you can see and enter the Kingdom of God?

Then check out this website and Gods4Me.com/Meet-Jesus and follow the steps through, then come back and pick up where you left off!

If you are already born again and have an understanding of your relationship with Jesus Christ, then read on and get ready to unlock some secrets, doors and keys to the Kingdom of God that will fuel and ignite your walk, mission and purpose from this day forward!

Preface

Several years back I wrote a book called "Thy Kingdom Come"; it is about a financial Kingdom revelation and a prevailing over the economic swings of the worlds economic system. When I received this revelation that no matter what is going on in the world, I can operate in, and reap benefits of an entirely different system, it changed my world in too many ways to go into here. I will review and discuss this when we get to the economic system of this worlds kingdom later on in the book. There are several great men of God that helped me to come to what some say is a very profound and certainly life changing shift.

I came to realize after some time that what I had was only a partial glimpse into the Kingdom of God and its ways. So my next few years was a quest for knowledge regarding the very important subject of the Kingdom of God. In the morning I would pray (and still do) for God to open my eyes to His Kingdom and help me not only to understand, but to be a conduit of what Jesus came to restore; in the evening I pray that He endow me with wisdom and understanding concerning the Kingdom and with all humbleness I say that He has been doing so. Countless nights He's woke me up at 3:00 +/- AM and just poured into me.. There were days where I woke up late for work because He had me up all night!

Now this world is not getting better on its own. In fact, the bible lays out and God shows us that this will get inevitably worse until the day Jesus returns. Christians will be hated for His Namesake, will be persecuted and even put to death. Jesus says that unless those days were cut short, no man would survive (Mathew 24:22). My brothers and sisters, I am sure you do not need a revelation to know that the last days and end time events are upon us. Mathew 24 is come alive, and as you look at the news it is like watching Johns Revelation and the book of Daniel unfold before our eyes at exponential degrees. It can be frightening if you do not know the Lord Jesus Christ personally.

What does that have to do with the Kingdom of God? In this book, I want to explain this worlds system (kingdom) and Gods system (Kingdom) and the reciprocity and contrast in their ways of operation. I want to share the wonderful revelations and understandings that I have come into and equally, I want you to know how to literally be in this world, in the midst of everything going on, but not be affected by it, because you know how to operate in a Kingdom and realm that literally supersedes the physical laws, principles and everything you think you know and understand about this world. I want to expound to you everything I've learned thus far about the Kingdom you may not know. The Kingdom of God.

Jesus was born of a virgin, walked on water, walked through walls, transported in time/space, manifested coins from fish, raised the dead, performed multiple miracles, healed the sick and even raised Himself up from the dead! He transcended the economic, political, social systems, and even ignored the laws of physics that we think we know! The systems of this world had no hold on Him and no authority except what He Himself permitted... Did you know that He became man and walked this earth and was put to death just so you can be restored to this level of power and authority? This is not a new revelation, but an understanding of what Jesus Himself said and demonstrated, and I am about to show you through the pages of this book.. Are you ready to live and operate on a level that most do not even recognize exist? Are you ready to live in this world and transcend its natural laws as if you live in a different reality? If you are ready to have an impact made on your life, and truly walk and live in the Kingdom of God while on this earth, then read on!

I wrote this book with building chapters; in that one builds on the next, from the foundation to the roof (then through it!). Some parts may seem elementary or tedious, and some redundant, but I promise you that if you will walk with me through the end of this book, your thinking will be transformed and your actions and life results will follow.

John 16:16
> *Jesus said that "The law and the prophets were until John: since that time the kingdom of God is preached, and every man presseth into it."*

The Amplified says it this way: "The Law and the [writings of the] Prophets were proclaimed until John; since then the gospel of the kingdom of God has been *and* continues to be preached, and everyone tries forcefully to go into it."

Jesus came proclaiming the Kingdom that He came to restore and everywhere He went, He brought and demonstrated that Kingdom.. This being so, and considering that Jesus said that this Kingdom will continue to be preached, shouldn't we not only understand, but be the best Ambassadors of the Kingdom that we can be? After all, Jesus also said

John 14:12
> *Verily, verily, I say unto you, He that believeth on me, the works that I do shall he do also; and greater works than these shall he do; because I go unto my Father*

Well, it's time!

What is a Kingdom?

Before you can run, we need to walk; before I can build an understanding, we must have a foundation to build on. Consequently, we cannot talk about kingdoms without an understanding of what kingdoms are, what's their purpose, how they function and how they impact the lives of its citizens, subjects, and places of rule or dominion.

To understand the Kingdom of God, we need a basic understanding of an earthly kingdom and how it operates. An earthly kingdom is a territory or domain governed by a king. He has absolute rule, authority and influence over a people and has a responsibility to his subjects for their wellbeing. His dominion and authority are sovereign and absolute. The Kingdom of God is no different.

I will get more into the attributes of the King later on, but what's important to know as we start off, is that all kings personally own the physical domain over which they reign. Kings and their area of dominion go together! We here in America have a hard time fully understanding this because we have a President, elected by the people to govern as the people choose (within the guidelines of our Constitution), and a King is sovereign, he is not voted into position and his rule is absolute... The entire area he rules is usually also called by his name. The very name of the king would depict the dominion... e.g. You would see in the movies even how that land or kingdom of Alexander the Great was vast, the kingdom of Genghis Khan was greater than any other earthly king.. The area of dominion, or their kingdom, was always tied to their name.. So it is with the Kingdom of God.

Everything under Gods absolute rule is in the Kingdom.

Dictionary.com defines kingdom as follows:

Kingdom   [king-d*u*h*m]

> Definition of *kingdom*
>
> *noun*
>
> 1. a state or government having a king or queen as its head.
> 2. anything conceived as constituting a realm or sphere of independent action or control: *the kingdom of thought.*
> 3. a realm or province of nature, especially one of the three broad divisions of natural objects: *the animal, vegetable, and mineral kingdoms.*
> 4. *Biology.* a taxonomic category of the second highest rank, just below domain: in a traditional five-kingdom classification scheme, separate kingdoms are assigned to animals (Animalia), plants (Plantae), fungi (Fungi), protozoa and eukaryotic algae (Protista), and bacteria (Monera).
> 5. the spiritual sovereignty of God or Christ.
> 6. the domain over which the spiritual sovereignty of God or Christ extends, whether in heaven or on earth.

Take another look at number 6: The domain over which the spiritual sovereignty of God or Christ extends, whether in heaven or on earth. The domain, which is the realm or place that the sovereignty, or dominance of God extends. Let me make it even more plain... It is any place where God has total rule or authority. Remember this point for later when we speak on authority, but for now understand the kings rule is the place where his power and authority extends and as a result, he owns.

A kingdom, which we understand to be a land under the rule or headship of a King (or Queen) is also called or known as a Monarchy. Monarchy was at one time the only form of leadership and was considered a very efficient form of government in its prime of existence. After all, it is much simpler to have one ruler make all the decisions. The trouble is, people who genuinely believe they have a divine mandate to rule over other people tend to be a bit unstable, become narcissistic, prideful and that's not to mention all that incestuous inbreeding to keep the monarchy preserved had to leave consequences that molded most of most ruthless rulers in history.

The rise of the desire for social equality and classlessness brought the rise of Democracy which started complicating things for the Kings and more countries rebelled. People started realizing that a divine mandate can't really feed them or save them from getting killed in a pointless war over who's grandma had a bigger claim on some piece of land nobody knows or cares about, except the guys whose grandmas started the whole thing.

The English were among first to test the waters of regicide among European nations, when Oliver Cromwell beheaded Charles I for treason in 1649. Although the monarchy (kingdom) was restored just 11 years later, the cat was out of the bag.

Revolutions in the 18th century shook the monarchies (kingdoms) all over the continent. French got fed up with their King in 1792 and decided to use him and his wife as test subjects for one of the most popular revolutionary inventions, the guillotine. In general, it is all downhill from there for all Kings and Queens in European countries.

As of today there are 10 kingdoms or monarchies left in the world that have a King or a Queen.

1. **The Kingdom of the Netherlands**
2. **The Kingdom of Spain**
3. **The Kingdom of Denmark**
4. **The Kingdom of Norway**
5. **The Kingdom of Bhutan**
6. **The Kingdom of Jordan**
7. **The Kingdom of Sweden**
8. **The Kingdom of Morocco**
9. **The Kingdom of Belgium**
    1. Ruling monarch: King Philippe
    2. House: Saxe-Coburg and Gotha
    3. Belgium and the UK share the same royal House, only the British branch changed the name to Windsor during the First World War. King Philippe of Belgium ascendant to the throne in 2013, when his father King Albert abdicated due to health issues.
10. **Kingdom of United Kingdom**
    1. House: Windsor
    2. Apart from the United Kingdom of Great Britain and Northern Ireland, Elizabeth II is also the queen of Australia, Jamaica, Antigua and Barbuda, Bahamas, Barbados, Belize, Canada, Grenada, New Zealand, Saint Kitts and Nevis, Saint Lucia, Saint Vincent and the Grenadines, Solomon Islands, and Tuvalu. In fact, she is the queen of so many countries that this list could consist of just her.

Just a side note for those who study the end times... It is odd that the majority of these countries are also in the 10 original countries to form and join the European Union in 1993, which many, myself included for a while assumed was related to the ten end times countries which would give their power to the anti-christ. (Daniel 7:7-8, Revelation 17:9-11) This book is not about that so do your own studies!

Americans were never too fond of kingdom monarchies, especially since King George decided that colonies must drink tea and pay taxes without the representation. *This rebellion although justified plays a role in our (Americans) understanding of authority that we will get into more later.* So it is because America is a Constitutional Republic, that is also a Democracy (a bit confusing for most), that I elaborate of the differences a little more than those residing in the UK or other monarchies would require.

Let's get back to the basics of a kingdom or monarchy...

We now know that a kingdom or monarchy is a form of government in which total sovereignty is invested in one person, a head of state called a monarch (King or Queen), who holds the position until death or abdication. Monarchs usually both hold and achieve their position through the right of hereditary succession (e.g., they were related, often the son or daughter, of the previous monarch).

Being that the papacy is a sovereign rule, it is also considered a monarchy and is sometimes called an elective monarchy.

There have also been hereditary rulers who weren't considered monarchs, such as the Stadtholders of Holland. Many monarchs have invoked religious reasons, such as being chosen by God, as a justification for their rule. Courts are often considered a key aspect of monarchies. These occur around the monarchs and provide a social meeting place for monarch and nobility.

In today's world, it's typical for monarchs, in a democracy, "to reign but not rule." This means that the monarch, whatever his or her title, serves as symbolic ruler but does not make policy, leaving it to the (indirectly) elected Prime Minister. However, in a few places, such as Saudi Arabia, kings (called *malik* in Arabian) really do have great influence over government policy. A "constitutional monarch," who reigns but does not rule, may be an emperor—as in Japan—or a king or queen, or theoretically any kind of monarch, terms have been used in many ways over the centuries.

So a king is one kind of monarch, so is an emperor. Monarchs are usually kings and emperors but they can sometimes be princes, dukes, sultans, or other titles. When we speak emperors, they typically rule empires and when we speak of kings, they rule kingdoms.

So for clarity and consistency, when we speak of kingdoms, we do so with the understanding and from the understanding of a single king with absolute sovereign rule over the kingdom and everything within.

II

Why Does it Matter?

As you now know and have a basic understanding of an earthly kingdom and how it operates, realize that every kingdom must have a king, also that it is true that every king is automatically a "lord". A lord is defined as *someone having power, authority, or influence; a master or ruler.* It is this quality of lordship that distinguishes a king from a president, a prime minister, a mayor or a governor. In fact, a king's lordship makes him different from any other kind of human leader. Lordship is what makes the king unique.

The most common word in scripture is the word "lord". Keep in mind that this word does not exist in a democracy, socialist society or a republic except for the word landlord, in reference to the one who owns and rents land to others. Landlord is the only common remnant of kingdoms in modern government and Western societies; but this concept of lord is one of the fundamental principles of a kingdom as you have already learned.

Now let me reiterate that king's sovereignty is absolute. He isn't voted into nor out of office or power. His sovereignty is by birthright--or should I say a right of birth. The same is true of a king's lordship. All kings are automatically lords, but not all lords are kings!

Keep this in mind--a king relates to dominion, while a lord relates to domain. The word dominion refers to the king's authority--his power. The word domain refers to the territory, the property, the geographical area over which his authority extends. A king exercises his authority over a specific geographical area. Keep in mind: A dominion refers to a king's authority and a domain refers to his geographical territory.

Remember that kings personally own the physical domain over which they reign. That makes them not only kings but also lords. Kings and property go together!

OK.. here we go! Now that we have that little understanding and foundation under our belts, I can begin to build the blocks of why all this is important to you, how it relates to your life and walk as a Christian and how to make it work for you. Let's start at the beginning and take a look at the first Kingdom set up by God Himself....

In the beginning God created the heaven and the earth.

> *² And the earth was without form, and void; and darkness was upon the face of the deep. And the Spirit of God moved upon the face of the waters.*

> *³ And God said, Let there be light: and there was light.*

Now, I am sure, or rather I trust that you are far enough in your walk with Christ that you know that God makes nothing that is without purpose and void, right?

From the time period known as "the beginning", God the Father, Jesus Christ, and the Holy Spirit always existed. There has never been a time when they did not exist. The "beginning" referred to in verse one, is the time in which God created the heavens and the earth. The "heavens" refers to the heavens surrounding the earth, including all of the galaxies, and the Milky Way, which is the particular solar system the earth belongs to. The earth was created at the same time the heavens were created.

If we were to outline Genesis 1, verse 1 describes the original creation. Verse 2 describes the earth in chaos; "without form, and void." Verse 3 begins an entire section that continues until Genesis 2:3, describing the restoration of the earth.

Everything God does is good and perfect (Psalm 18:30, James 1:17), so logic and just knowing God would allow us to deduce that when Jesus said in Luke 10:18 - "And he said unto them, I beheld Satan as lightning fall from heaven." That this period of time must have been somewhere between Genesis 1:1 and Genesis 1:2. Many biblical scholars agree and its commonly known as the gap theory that In the beginning God created the heaven and the earth... many years may have passed between then and Genesis 1:2.

God created the earth in beauty. He never creates anything "without form and void." Yet, in verse 2 the earth is described as being "without form, and void." There is no light upon the earth in verse two. The earth is under a tremendous curse. But in verse 3, God brings restoration to the earth, literally known as the six days of creation.

The earth was not created in six days. The earth was created instantaneously in a split second of time. During the six days of restoration, God took the earth, restored it, and made it beautiful again. God made it habitable for mankind. The history of man goes back some six thousand years. This is approximately the time when Adam was placed upon the earth. The earth itself is much older than six thousand years.

Scientist say the earth is 4.5 billion years old, we have no biblical account for the prehistoric age or many of the pre-Adamic times, nor do we have a biblical timeline for these events. So it may stand as reason that God did re-create the world in 6 days or 6 thousand years. The history of mankind is short in comparison to the age of the earth. One thing is certain, the earth existed long before the creation of Adam and Eve.

Isaiah 45:18 even tells us that God did not create the earth "without form and void." But something happened between verses one and two of Genesis chapter one, to cause the earth to move into the area of chaos. The Word of God gives a description of what happened to cause the chaos. Isaiah 14:12-15 gives a description of what the earth was like when it was originally created.

So let's see the big picture... God made earth to be a mirror image of heaven, created the moon to reflect the sun and man in His own image to reflect Himself here on earth. Heaven *is* my throne, and earth *is* my footstool:... (Acts 7:49)... everything on earth is refashioned to be a re-flection of what already is in heaven.. Jesus taught us to pray *Thy will be done on earth as it is in heaven*...

I will not go down verse by verse into the creation because this is not my mission but let's jump to verse 27,,,

> [27] *So God created man in his own image, in the image of God created he him; male and female created he them.*
>
> [28] *And God blessed them, and God said unto them, Be fruitful, and multiply, and replenish the earth, and subdue it: and have dominion over the fish of the sea, and over the fowl of the air, and over every living thing that moveth upon the earth.*
>
> [29] *And God said, Behold, I have given you every herb bearing seed, which is upon the face of all the earth, and every tree, in the which is the fruit of a tree yielding seed; to you it shall be for meat.*
>
> [30] *And to every beast of the earth, and to every fowl of the air, and to every thing that creepeth upon the earth, wherein there is life, I have given every green herb for meat: and it was so.*

³¹ And God saw every thing that he had made, and, behold, it was very good. And the evening and the morning were the sixth day.

God creates man from and in the earth in His own image; in fact chapter 2 verse 7 sheds more light on it and states: And the Lord God formed man of the dust of the ground, and breathed into his nostrils the breath of life; and man became a living soul. The original text translates that man became another speaking spirit. Verse 8 says that the Lord God planted a garden eastward in Eden; and there he put the man whom he had formed. Who planted the garden? God did. This is what was known as the Garden of Eden.

In Chapter 1 verse 28 above God gives man the very first command: *Be fruitful, and multiply, and replenish the earth, and subdue it: and have dominion over the fish of the sea, and over the fowl of the air, and over every living thing that moveth upon the earth.* Take special note to it... be fruitful... multiply... replenish the earth (pure fact that He says RE-plenish confirms that something was already "plenishing" at one time before) , subdue it.. in other words moderate or manage it – and have dominion over every living thing.. that's everything from trees, to animals, fish and even organisms we can't see.. It was Gods command and mans task to have dominion over this earth and to replenish everything outside the garden.

Now, the entire earth was Adams Kingdom, given to Him by God Himself. God said have dominion over the earth, not just the garden that God planted. So it is Mans task to take what is good and perfect in the garden and expand the Kingdom of God in to his own as to fill the entire earth with Gods Glory.

Now we know that at this time, there is no distance between heaven and earth, and God and man. Heaven is Gods throne, the earth is His footstool (Acts 7:49). There is no difference between God and man because there is no distance between God and man. I am not saying man was

God, but I am saying that God gave man the ability to rule in this world by the vehicle of his voice and command the fish of the sea, foul of the air and everything that has life because God gave him authority and power to do so... This is evidenced by the scriptures we just read. Gods command to man is to expand the Kingdom of God on earth (replenish the earth) and way he would do it is through the dominion God gave him.

Can you picture it? In my mind, I see what I envision heaven being like, here on earth... no such thing as entropy, nothing dies, decays or withers. Everything is in its full glory and blossoming with a bouquet of colors that are unimaginable! Never a cloud in the sky (there was no rain) and all the animals and creatures got along.. Adam was even able to communicate with them and speak to them while they obeyed his voice because he had total dominion over everything in the earth! It was Adams task to take everything that was good and perfect in this garden and expand it to the rest of the world.. Can you see the picture?

Adam ruled and ordered not by the sweat of his brow, not by working with his hands even, but by the vehicle of his voice... He spoke and it happened.. He commanded and nature obeyed, because God gave him dominion. What a wonderful picture! And then because it was so filled with the glory of Gods Kingdom here on earth, God Himself would even come down and converse with Adam, face to face... What a perfect place this earth was!

Gen 3:8 lets us know that God would walk with Adam in the garden and speak with him as you and I would speak... He was able to do this because both God and man were in one accord, in agreement and harmony, and thus, there was no distance (spiritually) between them. So we have God in heaven, and earth as its reflection; God the Father and man as His reflection (made in His image). There was congruency between heaven and earth, between the Kingdom of God in heaven and earth and thus no distance between God and man... everything was as the Kingdom of Heaven here on earth.. UNTIL...

The serpent, who we know is the devil, confronts Eve and tricks her into eating from the one tree God said not to eat of. Then she gave it to her husband Adam to eat, who in his eating disobeyed Gods command.

> Verse 6 -*And when the woman saw that the tree was good for food, and that it was pleasant to the eyes, and a tree to be desired to make one wise, she took of the fruit thereof, and did eat, and gave also unto her husband with her; and he did eat.*
>
> *⁷ And the eyes of them both were opened, and they knew that they were naked; and they sewed fig leaves together, and made themselves aprons.*
>
> *⁸ And they heard the voice of the Lord God walking in the garden in the cool of the day: and Adam and his wife hid themselves from the presence of the Lord God amongst the trees of the garden.*

And the physical eyes of them both were opened, and they knew that they were naked... were their eyes physically closed before? No, but just as we now only see certain color or light spectrums and so it was with them, on a different level. So now they are acquainted with sin through the eye-gates that they opened up in their disobedience. God comes walking in the garden and knowing fully where Adam was and what happened asks.. *"Adam, where art thou?.."* I believe the question was not so much God asking where he was physically, but more of Adam, where are you? What happened to the Adam that I created? But Adam responds with the fact that he was afraid because he knew he was naked and hid himself... This is the first time we see fear introduced in the bible, and it is a direct result of Adams sin. The very first consequence of mans sin is fear being introduced.

Then God said: "..*Who told thee that thou wast naked? Hast thou eaten of the tree, whereof I commanded thee that thou shouldest not eat?"* rather than take responsibility and repent, fear causes Adam to blame, Eve, then Eve blames the serpent... Then comes the judgment from God on the matter:

> *¹⁴ And the Lord God said unto the serpent, Because thou hast done this, thou art cursed above all cattle, and above every beast of the field; upon thy belly shalt thou go, and dust shalt thou eat all the days of thy life:*

> *¹⁵ And I will put enmity between thee and the woman, and between thy seed and her seed; it shall bruise thy head, and thou shalt bruise his heel.*

> *¹⁶ Unto the woman he said, I will greatly multiply thy sorrow and thy conception; in sorrow thou shalt bring forth children; and thy desire shall be to thy husband, and he shall rule over thee.*

> *¹⁷ And unto Adam he said, Because thou hast hearkened unto the voice of thy wife, and hast eaten of the tree, of which I commanded thee, saying, Thou shalt not eat of it: cursed is the ground for thy sake; in sorrow shalt thou eat of it all the days of thy life;*

> *¹⁸ Thorns also and thistles shall it bring forth to thee; and thou shalt eat the herb of the field;*

> *¹⁹ In the sweat of thy face shalt thou eat bread, till thou return unto the ground; for out of it wast thou taken: for dust thou art, and unto dust shalt thou return.*

This is important because God starts off with the first end time prophesy and even in Gods judgment, there is mercy. God's curse on the serpent, in particular, was laced with words of hope. The woman mentioned in Genesis 3:15 is Eve. The serpent, addressed directly, is the animal that Satan used to deceive the woman. Some of the curse was directed at the animal (verse 14); at the same time, the curse of God falls upon Satan, who had taken the serpent's form or body in Eden (cf. the dragon in Revelation 12:9).

As part of the curse, enmity—mutual hatred and ill will—will exist between the woman and the serpent. Later, the same enmity will continue between the woman's seed or offspring (mankind in general, since Eve is the "mother of all living," Genesis 3:20) and the serpent's seed. Their offspring will remain enemies throughout all generations. The serpent's (metaphorical) offspring are demonic forces and also those people who follow the devil and accomplish his will. Jesus called the Pharisees a "brood of vipers" in Matthew 12:34 and said they belonged to their "*father, the devil*" in John 8:44.

In short, God says that Satan will always be the enemy of mankind. It follows that people who side with Satan will be at perpetual war with God's elect and that we are engaged in a very real battle between good and evil (Ephesians 6:12).

Genesis 3:15 is a remarkable verse, often called the protoevangelium (literally, "first gospel"), because it is the Bible's first prediction of a Savior. The second half of the verse gives two messianic prophecies concerning that Savior:

The first messianic prophecy in Genesis 3:15 is that "*he will crush your head.*" That is, the seed of the woman will crush the serpent's head. The Amplified Bible makes it clear that "*the woman's seed*" is more than mankind in general; it is an individual representing all mankind:

> "*And I will put enmity* (open hostility) *Between you and the woman,*
> *And between your seed* (offspring) *and her Seed;*
> *He shall* [fatally] *bruise your head.*"

The second messianic prophecy in Genesis 3:15 is that *"you will strike his heel."* That is, the serpent will bite the heel of "the woman's seed." The heel-bite is set in contrast to the head-crush, as the Amplified Bible brings out: *"And you shall* [only] *bruise His heel."*

This passage points to the promise of Jesus' birth, His redemption, and His victory over Satan. The woman's offspring is Jesus. Being virgin-born, He is literally the offspring of a woman (Matthew 1:25; Galatians 4:4; cf. Isaiah 7:14). Being the Son of Man, He is the perfect representative of humankind. The devil's offspring were the evil men and demonic forces who, like a snake, lay in wait for the Savior and struck at Him. Their venomous conspiracy condemned Jesus to be crucified.

But the serpent's strike did not spell the end of the Offspring of the woman. Jesus rose the third day, breaking the power of death and winning the ultimate victory. With the cross, Jesus *"crushed"* the devil's head, defeating him forever. So, in Genesis 3:15, the crushing of the serpent's head was a picture of Jesus' triumph over sin and Satan at the cross (cf. John 12:31). The striking of the Messiah's heel was a picture of the wounding and death of Jesus on the cross. Satan bruised Jesus' *"heel,"* but Jesus showed complete dominance over Satan by bruising his *"head."*

Satan, although still active in this world, is a defeated foe. His doom is sure: "And the devil . . . was thrown into the lake of burning sulfur" (Revelation 20:10). Until that time, there remains enmity between Satan and God's children.

The prophetic protoevangelium shows us that God always had the plan of salvation in mind and informed us of His plan as soon as sin entered the world.

Satan framed a plan involving the serpent in Eden, but God was way ahead of him, having already ordained the Serpent-crusher. Jesus Christ perfectly fulfilled God's mission: *"The reason the Son of God appeared was to destroy the works of the devil"* (1 John 3:8).

OK, let's come full circle before I get ahead of myself!

When Adam transgressed, sin came into the world and the dominion that was given to Adam by God in the garden was lost. It was given over to Satan. This is similar to how we have constitutional and inalienable rights as a citizen in America, unless we chose to give up those rights. Well, Adam chose, by virtue of his disobedience, to give up his right of dominion over the land, sea and air. I hear many preachers preach that he gave up the earth... That is not the case; the earth is the Lords and the fullness thereof (Ps 24:1), it was never mans to give. Man lost his ability to have kingdom dominion, authority and to rule and reign as he did before. Now death, sickness, disease and all the laws of entropy are put into place along with all the other limiting laws of physics, and every other law outside of the Kingdom of God. This will be important to remember as we get more into Kingdom Authority later.

So to recap, God created the earth to be a reflection of the Kingdom of Heaven. Then planted the Garden (another reflection) and created man in His image and likeness to be a reflection of Himself, here on earth and to expand that Kingdom that He created in earth (reflecting heaven) and, until the whole earth is filled with His Glory (Isaiah 6:2-3). I watched an interview done with Dr. Miles Monroe and he was asked about the Kingdom of God and its Glory... The response he gave was simple but profound: He picked up a blooming rose bud from the vase next to him and said do you see this? Do you see this rose bud blooming? Well this is like the Kingdom of God, the full glory of the rose is inside this bud, but you can't see it all yet. The glory is inside.. When it is at its fullest bloom, the flower is said to be in its glory! That's how the expanding Kingdom of God is here on earth!

So why didn't God zap Eve with a lightning bolt, squash Adam and start all over again? Because God is not on plan B... He knew what would happen before it happened and assigned the end before the beginning. Mans fall and subsequent redemption and everything happening is all part of Gods first, plan A, one and only design! As we saw in Genesis 3:15, God already had a redemptive plan!

Why are you here? What's your purpose? Let's shortcut every secular philosophy class and theory of being and get to the answer to the age old question... Who am I and why am I here? Well, I would say that I answered that question already for you.. God created man and placed him in the garden that He planted and told man to "... *Be fruitful, and multiply, and replenish the earth, and subdue it: and have dominion...*" You should have this down at this point.. God wants man to be a re-flection of Him and to have dominion over the earth and to replenish it with His Glory. Herein is your chief purpose!!!!

But there was a challenge that needed to be overcome. Adam gave it away. He gave away his dominion through this realm. Being that there are laws now in place that God will not transgress, because it would violate his own laws and void out the plan, God had to act from within the system to change the system and revert the dominion back to man so man can once again "... *Be fruitful, and multiply, and replenish the earth, and subdue it: and have dominion...*" So that's where He foretold of the prophetic events of Genesis 3:15.

John 3:16

> *For God so loved the world, that he gave his only begotten Son, that whosoever believeth in him should not perish, but have ever-lasting life.*

If your purpose is what I explained above, and God so loved you that He gave His only begotten Son for you.. What was His purpose? Why did Jesus have to come to earth? Let's get bible answers for this..

1 John 3:8

> He that committeth sin is of the devil; for the devil sinneth from the beginning. For this purpose the Son of God was manifested, that he might destroy the works of the devil.

Matthew 18:11

> For the Son of man is come to **save that which was lost.**

The Gospel of Luke states it this way...

Luke 19:10

> For the Son of man is come to **seek and to save _that_ which was lost.**

Notice the scripture does not say those, or them who were lost. The word "that" is a definite article... So what was "that" which was lost? What was it that Jesus came to save? (I am hoping that being this far into the book and your understanding you can answer this rhetorical question!)

If you guessed the Kingdom, you guessed correct!

So I will bypass the Old Testament being a foreshadow and precursor to the New for the sake of time and for the fact that that is not a part of this teaching, but one that every Christian should study out. God gave Commandments, Laws and Prophets to always lead to the supposition of the coming of His Son Jesus Christ and the redemptive power of the cross and everything leading to it and succeeding it.

We should always remember that Jesus always focused on the Kingdom.. so when He is of the age of 30 years and lawfully able to go into ministry, He goes to His cousin older (by 6 months) John, who is already in ministry and baptizing people in the Jordan...

Mathew 3 starts out:

In those days came John the Baptist, preaching in the wilderness of Judaea,

*² And saying, **Repent ye: for the kingdom of heaven is at hand.***

Then in verse 11 comes Jesus...

> *¹¹ I indeed baptize you with water unto repentance. but he that cometh after me is mightier than I, whose shoes I am not worthy to bear: he shall baptize you with the Holy Ghost, and with fire:*
>
> *¹² Whose fan is in his hand, and he will throughly purge his floor, and gather his wheat into the garner; but he will burn up the chaff with unquenchable fire.*
>
> *¹³ Then cometh Jesus from Galilee to Jordan unto John, to be baptized of him.*
>
> *¹⁴ But John forbad him, saying, I have need to be baptized of thee, and comest thou to me?*
>
> *¹⁵ And Jesus answering said unto him, Suffer it to be so now: ....*

Jesus comes out of the desert and we read in Mathew Chapter 4:

> *¹⁷ From that time Jesus began to preach, and to say, Repent: for the kingdom of heaven is at hand.*

Jesus stated in Luke 16:16

> *The law and the prophets were until John: <u>**since that time the**</u>*
> <u>**kingdom of God is preached,**</u> *and every man presseth into it.*

Matthew 4:23

> *And Jesus went about all Galilee, teaching in their synagogues,*
> <u>*and preaching the gospel of the kingdom, and healing all manner*</u>
> <u>*of sickness and all manner of disease among the people.*</u>

Before we go deeper into this rabbit hole can you see it? Can you see the beginning, the middle and the end? Do you see that Jesus came to restore a Kingdom? He came to restore mans dominion here on earth so we (you and I) can continue to have dominion and subdue the earth and expand the Kingdom of God here on earth? In fact.. When the disciples asked Jesus to show them how to pray... He said to pray this way:

Mathew 6

> *⁹ After this manner therefore pray ye: Our Father which art in heaven, Hallowed be thy name.*

> *¹⁰ <u>Thy Kingdom come, Thy will be done in earth, as it is in heaven.</u>*

> *¹¹ Give us this day our daily bread.*

> *¹² And forgive us our debts, as we forgive our debtors.*

> *¹³ And lead us not into temptation, but deliver us from evil: <u>For thine is the Kingdom, and the power, and the glory, for ever.</u> Amen.*

So here we read Jesus saying to pray **Thy Kingdom Come**.. This is the thesis of the prayer.. That Gods Kingdom will come on earth, as it already is in heaven. (sound familiar?) Then we see at the end of the prayer, Jesus wraps it up by reiterating the beginning in saying *"For*

Thine is the Kingdom, the power, and the glory".... And we understand by this, that He is also showing us the order of things in the Kingdom... Kingdom leads to Power and Power leads to Glory...And we have people who have not understood the process that the Kingdom of God begins as a seed, and ends in Glory... Because when you seek the Power, or the Glory, without seeking the Kingdom first, you have Chaos and disorder – Anarchy .

Unless the Kingdom comes, which directly effects earth and brings it into alignment with heaven, His will cannot be done, and then there cannot be a release of Power, and His Glory is not released. The Kingdom starts with people pressing into it... and ends (culminates) in Glory... If you want to see Glory, press into the Kingdom... **For the earth shall be filled with the knowledge of the glory of the LORD, as the waters cover the sea.**

When we seek the Kingdom to be here on earth, it is Gods will, and when we do Gods will, He will give us the Power, and when we have the Power, we will see the Glory; this is why we are to seek FIRST the Kingdom of God (Mat 6:33). We need an understanding of the Kingdom of God today...

Luke 16:16

> *The law and the prophets were until John: <u>since that time the kingdom of God is preached,</u> and every man presseth into it.*

Matthew 4:23

> *And Jesus went about all Galilee, teaching in their synagogues, and preaching the gospel of the kingdom, and healing all manner of sickness and all manner of disease among the people.*

This is what Jesus preached and in fact, that's all the disciples preached.. Jesus preached the Kingdom and they preached Jesus! What did they preach? Acts 10:38 *How God anointed Jesus of Nazareth with the Holy Ghost and with power: who went about doing good, and healing all that were oppressed of the devil; for God was with him.* It's the Gospel of the Kingdom!

So why isn't every church Pastor, Teacher Evangelist, Apostle and Prophet teaching on the Kingdom? This is what Jesus preached.. in fact, its ALL He preached.. and everywhere He went, He demonstrated the Kingdom with signs following. The miracles are just a manifestation of the Kingdom. When you step into the Kingdom, for real, miracles follow because Power follows and it will culminate in Glory.

The enemy tried to stop the Kingdom from advancing back in the garden, and he's been trying ever since. So we have churches today teaching 7 ways to be happy and how to overcome strife but nowhere (or very few places) are preaching the Kingdom in its fullness, and truly transforming the world around them though their ministries. Please do not mistake my words for criticism of the Church; it is not an indictment, but a correction. With 250 years of religious freedom in America we should be walking on water by now instead of building electric cars!

When you have an understanding of the Kingdom, how it operates, and you possess a working knowledge of your rights as a citizen of the Kingdom, every facet of your known natural reality will change, because in the Kingdom, everything in this natural world is subject to change. And Jesus Christ is the proof!

III

Anatomy of a Kingdom

The Kingdom concept was born in the heart of man, placed there by his Creator as the purpose for which he was created. Despite the fact that there were many types of kingdoms throughout history, there are certain characteristics common to all kingdoms. The Kingdom of God also possesses these components. Here are some of them, so that you can understand the Kingdom concept:

Anatomy of a Kingdom

- King
- Realm or Territory
- Government (Constitution)
- A Governor
- Citizens
- Laws
- Privileges / Rights
- Economic System
- Culture
- Language
- Security (army)

The King

The King is the embodiment of the kingdom, representing its glory and nature. The kingdom is a reflection of the king. If the king is evil and corrupt, his kingdom will be evil and corrupt. If the king is honorable, truthful and kind, his kingdom will be also. Authority flows from the king and the word of the king is supreme.

God is the King of the supernatural realm called Heaven. It is invisible but very real. Heaven is more real than the natural realm in which we live, breathe and exist. All things flow from this Heavenly realm and therefore it is the source of the natural realm and the reason mankind exists.

God's original plan and purpose was to extend His heavenly kingdom on earth. It was to bring His invisible supernatural rule into the visible natural world. It was for this reason that He created mankind—male and female. He created them in His own image and clothed them in physical bodies of flesh, bone and blood from the dirt of this earth. He created them to exercise dominion over the earth just as He does in Heaven. Mankind was to be His representative, or Ambassador, ruling here one earth in His name and under His authority. Keep in mind; this was all before the fall of mankind, meaning his disobedience to the King's command.

The Lord God created man in His own image and likeness and He was King. Adam was appointed to be a king as well. As king of the earth, Adam possessed certain unique qualities and characteristics that set him apart from all other creatures on this earth. One of those qualities is the power of choice, free will. Mankind was created with the ability to reason—to frame his own thoughts and ideas and make decisions. In this, he was like his Creator.

Because Adam sinned and gave up his right to the Kingdom dominion, we had an issue in that God still has a plan for the earth, His Kingdom and man that did not change.

We also understand according to Romans 11:29 that the gifts and calling of the Lord are irrevocable.

> *For the gifts and the calling of God are irrevocable [for He does not withdraw what He has given, nor does He change His mind about those to whom He gives His grace or to whom He sends His call].* AMP

What do I mean by that?

The Lord God's original plan and purpose were still in place. Mankind's destiny was to rule the earth. He had to retrieve his Kingdom back. When the time was right in history (the bible calls it the fullness of time), the King of Heaven sent His Son to reestablish Heaven's rule here. He sent His Son to restore man to his earthly Kingdom.

John 3:16

> *For God so loved the world that He gave His only begotten Son, that whoever believes in Him should not perish but have everlasting life.*

The Lord Jesus was proclaiming one simple message: From that time Jesus began to preach and to say, "Repent, for the Kingdom of Heaven is at hand." Matthew 4:17 – In other words, the Kingdom is back! The King is back!

Jesus came as the second Adam, or the last Adam or we can say, as the second King on earth to replace and restore all that the first earthly king lost.

In Isaiah 9:6, which is a prophetic scripture foretelling the birth of Jesus, God says " For unto us a Child is born, Unto us a Son is given; And the government will be upon His shoulder...."What government is He talking about? If you said Gods government or the Kingdom of God, you're correct! He came as a King to restore the Kingdom!

I can give many examples but for the sake of not being too redundant, I'll give the most profound:

John 18:36-37

> *Jesus said to Pilate, '**My kingdom is not of this world.** If my kingdom were of this world, my servants would have been fighting, that I might not be delivered over to the Jews. But my kingdom is not from the world.'*
>
> *Then Pilate said to Jesus, 'So you are a king, are you?' Jesus answered, '**You say that I am a king. For this I was born, and for this I have come into the world,** to bear witness to the truth'."*

Remember, Adam was created as king and ruler of this earth; he sinned and caused the fall, then Jesus is the King of the Kingdom who came to restore the dominion to man as His earthly Ambassadors and He gave us the Keys to the Kingdom before departing to continue the reign. And because earth is to be a reflection of heaven, you are essentially ambassadors, or kings here on earth that rule over the kingdom of earth and report to the King of kings in the Kingdom of Heaven.

The Territory

The King and Kingdom are concepts that are of heavenly origin, not earthly origin. The Lord God chose those concepts to describe His plan for mankind on this earth.

The Territory is the domain over which the king exercises total authority. The territory and its resources and people

are all personal property of the king. In a kingdom, everything in it belongs to the King; the king by right, owns all and, therefore, is considered lord over all. Keep in mind, the word lord denotes ownership by right. Lord is only given to one who is sovereign owner.

This is why the Scripture declares in Psalm 24:1 *The earth is the Lord's, and everything in it. The world and all its people belong to Him.*

So Adam did not give up the earth, it was never his to give; he gave up his dominion and rule over it by virtue of submitting his will to the serpent in the garden. Th9iis means in reality, we own noting in this world... Not your house, car, boat, money or anything else that we call "ours" or "mine", it's all Gods. Always has been, always will be.

Unrelated Tidbit:

> *When we tithe and say we are giving God His 10%, we traditionally have the understanding that the rest is ours; but now you understand that none of it was ever ours, and you return 10% (or whatever you give), and He blesses the remainder of His money that he lets you hold and steward.*

So to summarize this: Jesus is the King and the government/Kingdom is upon His shoulders, and everything within the Kingdom belongs to Him, even the people (you and I).

Jesus said in John 16:7 that it is expedient for Him to go back to the Father so the He can send us another Comforter. That Person was/is the Holy Spirit, who is sent to be our Governor! We will discuss Him more later but it is important that you see the entire structure as we explain and illuminate it.

Government / The Constitution

Next thing we have in a Kingdom is the Constitution, which is the covenant of a king with his citizens and expresses the mind and will of the king for his citizens and the kingdom. It is the king's written governing laws, rights, and privileges for his people. Even in America we have a Constitution and a Bill of Rights that define all the rights an privileges of the citizens. Sadly because we live in what is known as a *Federal Constitutional Republic* (which is a cross of a republic and a democracy), ideologies of wayward elected officials would see this exterminated if they had their way.

The Bible contains the constitution of the Kingdom of God, which details His will and mind for His citizens. The Bible is God's Constitution--His Testaments--to His citizens in the Kingdom. And the good part is that God puts His Word above His Name and there is not one Word in the Bible that can be changed or erased, for all eternity!

Remember, the Lord God's Constitution isn't a religious book, but one of a legal nature. It is the Lord God's Testament to His people. We refer to it as the Bible--the origin of this word comes from the Greek name for a Phoenician city, *Byblos,* where papyrus, Bublos, was made and used to write the scriptures on scrolls. From that came the Latin word *Biblia*--book--which became holy book. In reality, it is the King's Constitution to all mankind!

I will delight in your decrees and not forget Your word. Psalm 119:16

So when you want to know what rights you have as a citizen of the Kingdom of God, open the Constitution and read how no weapon formed against you has the right to prosper, how sickness and disease have no right to your body and how a thief (the thief) when found must make restitution of 7-10 times what he stole! All your rights, privileges and promises are in the constitution and they are non-revocable and non-negotiable. The challenge many have is in understanding of application and enforcement so many go on claiming the rights but never experiencing the benefits... We are going to change that by the end of this book!

Governor

Every King has an appointed Governor, so what are some of the qualities of our Governor—the Holy Spirit?

The "Ambassador" Paul desired to instill the nature of the Heavenly Kingdom in the lives of the first century citizens of the Kingdom. They were learning what it meant to be aligned with the King. In his letter to the Kingdom citizens of Galatia, he laid out some characteristics of our King that should be manifest in us.

Galatians 5:22-25

> *But the Holy Spirit produces this kind of fruit in our lives: love, joy, peace, patience, kindness, goodness, faithfulness, gentleness, and self-control. There is no law against these things! Those who belong to Christ Jesus have nailed the passions and desires of their sinful nature to His cross and crucified them there. Since we are living by the Spirit, let us follow the Spirit's leading in every part of our lives.*

Any true manifestation of the Kingdom of the Lord God on this earth will definitely have those characteristics.

Paul referred to those qualities as "the fruit of the Spirit". Wherever our Governor—Holy Spirit—resides, those qualities should be operating indicating the culture of our King and His Kingdom is present. Paul used the analogy of fruit because he knew that it doesn't appear overnight. It must grow in fertile soil. Remember, we live in a fallen world. Fruit develops over time. He wanted us to know we would have to cultivate the culture of the King in our lives by the leading and guidance of the Holy Spirit.

Keep in mind, the Governor teaches us the nature of the original government in Heaven. After that, He shows us that because He lives within us, we have the original nature of our Lord and King and need to manifest it in our lives.

When you receive the Holy Spirit (our Governor) you also receive the seed of the Kingdom nature. Note that I said "seed". You must develop this seed by putting into your daily life elements of the Kingdom—the Lord God's Word and a fertile prayer life.

Here is an example of what I mean: An orange tree does not need to work to produce its fruit. The seeds of the fruit are within it and eventually, through a process of maturity, it is enabled by elements such as the nutrients in the earth and sunlight to grow nourishing fruit. What is on the inside of the orange becomes manifested on the branches. The seed brings forth the tree, branches and blossoms which grows the fruit. Without the proper nourishment and water the seed would die in the ground, never bringing forth the fruit!

It is the spiritual nutrients that enable our fruit to grow in our lives, maintaining a continued connection with our King. As I have mentioned earlier, it is by studying the Constitution of the Kingdom, which the world calls the Bible, which nourishes us. It is our life source in the Kingdom! Without it, our fruit will never grow and manifest in our lives and benefit those in our lives.

Also, you must yield to the leading and guidance of our Governor if you are to change. Remember, just as oranges are the natural product of an orange tree, so the fruit of the Spirit become a natural development in the life of citizens of the Lord God's Kingdom because we are reflecting the nature of our King.

Galatians 5:4-5

> *For if you are trying to make yourselves right with God by keeping the law, you have been cut off from Christ! You have fallen away from God's grace. But we who live by the Spirit eagerly wait to receive by faith the righteousness God has promised to us.*

Your fruit isn't only for your benefit, but for the benefit of those around you. It is the only way to truly represent the Kingdom to the world!

Galatians 5:16-21

> *This I say then, Walk in the Spirit, and ye shall not fulfil the lust of the flesh.*
>
> *For the flesh lusteth against the Spirit, and the Spirit against the flesh: and these are contrary the one to the other: so that ye cannot do the things that ye would.*
>
> *But if ye be led of the Spirit, ye are not under the law.*
>
> *Now the works of the flesh are manifest, which are these; Adultery, fornication, uncleanness, lasciviousness,*
>
> *Idolatry, witchcraft, hatred, variance, emulations, wrath, strife, seditions, heresies,*
>
> *Envyings, murders, drunkenness, revellings, and such like: of the which **I tell you before, as I have also told you in time past, that they which do such things shall not inherit the kingdom of God.***

Lastly, and of great importance, what I want you to see is that the empowerment that you now hold as a citizen of the Kingdom is manifested from the King (Jesus), through the Governor (the Holy Spirit) and into and though you, His Ambassador!

Jesus gave the disciples knowledge, affirmation and authority to perform the works of the Kingdom while He was here, but and then told them that it was expedient that He depart so that the Holy Spirit will come and endow them with Power. And then, somewhere in an upper room.. The Holy Spirit came to complete the assignment of the King and re-establish His Kingdom here on earth!

From that point on, miracles signs and wonders went forth, thousands of new citizens were added to the Kingdom daily, because the preached the Kingdom, in the Power and demonstration of the Kingdom; and this is what each citizen is called top do, because you are not only a citizen but an Ambassador!

Citizens

Every kingdom must have citizens! The citizenry is, collectively, the people that live under the rule of the king. Citizenship in a kingdom is not a right, but a privilege, and is a result of the king's choice.

The benefits and privileges of a kingdom are only accessible to citizens and therefore the favor of the king is always a privilege.

Once one becomes a citizen of the kingdom, all the rights of citizenship are at the citizen's pleasure. The king is obligated to care for and protect all of his citizens; and their welfare is a reflection on the king himself.

The number one goal of a citizen in a kingdom is to be subject to the king, seeking only to remain in right-standing with him. This is called righteousness. This is why Jesus said the priority of all men is to seek *first* His Kingdom. (Matthew 6:33)

So when you became born again, repented and submitted your life to the supreme rule and reign of Jesus Christ as King over your life, you became a citizen of the Kingdom of God. It's not a dual citizenship; the Kingdom of God is a higher (the highest) government there is and all other systems, kingdoms and realms are subject to its laws. What does that mean? It means you are an Ambassador for Christ the King

2 Corinthians 5:20

> *Now then we are ambassadors for Christ, as though God did beseech you by us: we pray you in Christ's stead, be ye reconciled to God.*

An Ambassador is a Diplomat of the Country or Kingdom from which he represents. As a Diplomat from the Kingdom of God here on earth, you have *Diplomatic Immunity* to many of the laws concerning this earth (As long as you are submitted to the Kingdom of God). The kingdom of this world is subject to you!

So when sickness, disease, infirmity or any destructive force of the world's system comes against you, you can rightfully reject it on the basis of Diplomatic Immunity! That sickness is from a kingdom that you are not a citizen of; you may reside there, but your citizenship is of another Kingdom. The natural laws (principles) of the kingdom of this world are ALL subject to the laws of the Kingdom of God, period.

This is the foundational parameter that permitted Jesus to walk on water, walk through walls, stop the wind and calm the sea and heal all oppressions of the enemy. His Kingdom was not of this world!

OK, get this, because the bible tells us in

Romans 8:11

> *But if the Spirit of him that raised up Jesus from the dead dwell in you, he that raised up Christ from the dead shall also quicken your mortal bodies by his Spirit that dwelleth in you.*

The SAME SPIRIT... that's your Governor, the one who leads you and guides you and has come into you with the Power of the King and the Kingdom! So now, there is nothing that Jesus did on this earth that you cannot do.. in fact,

John 14:12 says:

> *Verily, verily, I say unto you, He that believeth on me, the works that I do shall he do also; and greater works than these shall he do; because I go unto my Father.*

Do you see and realize the Power that is bestowed upon you as a Kingdom Ambassador?

You do not need to read any further if you really get this (but please do!), you can take the Keys and start exercising your dominion as of right and expanding the Kingdom today!

The Laws

Every Kingdom has its own law. This is not the Ten Commandments, but law that constitutes the standards and principles established by the king himself, by which his kingdom will function and be administered. The laws of a kingdom are to be obeyed by all, including foreigners residing in it.

The laws of the kingdom are the way by which one is guaranteed access to the benefits of the king and the kingdom. Violations of kingdom law place a citizen at odds with the king and thus interrupt the favorable position one enjoys with the king.

The laws in a kingdom cannot be changed by the citizens, nor are they subject to a culture change, citizen referendum or debate. Simply put, the word of the King is law in his kingdom. When the king put his signet or seal on a matter, it was done, forever and cannot be undone, even by the king himself!

Rebellion against the law is rebellion against the king. King David understood this principle of the royal word when he stated, in

Psalm 138:2-3

> *I bow before Your Holy Temple as I worship. I praise Your name for Your unfailing love and faithfulness; for Your promises are backed by all the honor of Your name. As soon as I pray, You answer me; You encourage me by giving me strength.*

A Code of Ethics is the acceptable conduct of the citizens in the kingdom and their representation of the kingdom. This code includes moral standards, social relationships, personal conduct, attitude, attire and manner of life. We will speak more about the laws and principles later in its own context.

Privileges / Rights

The Privileges are the benefits the king lavishes on his faithful citizens. This aspect of kingdom is very different from other forms of government. In a kingdom, citizenship is always desired by the people because, once you are in the kingdom, the king is personally responsible for you and your needs. In addition, because the king owns everything within his kingdom, he can give to any citizen any or all of his wealth as he desires.

There is a "common wealth" in the Kingdom. The King provides for His own! We don't "own" anything. It all belongs to the Lord God. He gives us access. A Commonwealth is described as *one founded on law and united by compact or tacit agreement of the people for the common good; one in which supreme authority is vested in the people.* It is the King's commitment to see that all of His citizens have equal access to the wealth and resources of the Kingdom. This is very important to the King because the quality of life of His citizens reflects the glory and reputation of the King. When the welfare of the King's citizens is excellent, then the reputation among other kings is honorable. All that is required is to seek after His Kingdom and His righteousness!

Matthew 6:25-34

Therefore I say to you, do not worry about your life, what you will eat or what you will drink; nor about your body, what you will put on. Is not life more than food and the body more than clothing? Look at the birds of the air, for they neither sow nor reap nor gather into barns; yet your heavenly Father feeds them. Are you not of more value than they? Which of you by worrying can add one cubit to his stature?

So why do you worry about clothing? Consider the lilies of the field, how they grow: they neither toil nor spin; and yet I say to you that even Solomon in all his glory was not arrayed like one of these. Now if God so clothes the grass of the field, which today is, and tomorrow is thrown into the oven, will He not much more clothe you, O you of little faith?

Therefore do not worry, saying, 'What shall we eat?' or 'What shall we drink?' or 'What shall we wear?' For after all these things the Gentiles seek. For your heavenly Father knows that you *need all these things. <u>But seek first the Kingdom of God and His</u> <u>righteousness, and all these things shall be added to you.</u> There-fore do not worry about tomorrow, for tomorrow will worry about its own things. Sufficient for the day is its own trouble.*

Once you've entered into citizenship of the Kingdom, and are submit-ted to its laws (that is, not to be in violation of any law), then everything and every area of your life is entitled to the rights and privileges of the Kingdom in those areas. Why do I say it like that? Because I believe you can have one part of your life fully submitted to the Kingdom of God, and not others, areas that we hold out on hoping they'd be non-applicable and God will look the other way. And He will (to an extent), because of the Love and Grace of Jesus Christ, but the benefits that would be applicable under the Kingdom Law in that area, would also now be non-applicable to your life. In example, if I submit my finances to God and put Him first in this area, He will bless me in this area and supply my financial needs (We will speak more on that later), and if I submit my mind to the Lord and do not give in to anger, arguing and contention then He will bless me with peace, but If I am not submitted in the area of my health and I drink excess alcohol, I cannot claim the right to healing in my liver when it fails as a result, unless I repent and submit that to Him, then He is faithful and just to forgive me of my sins and heal me.

I know that's hard to grasp for many because we are taught that when you come to Christ everything is going to be roses, cotton candy and ice cream dandy but it's simply not true. You cannot claim Kingdom prom-ises and ignore Kingdom principles. Anything not under the Kingdom umbrella gets wet. But let's go a bit further: take special note to verse 33 above: *But seek first the Kingdom of God and His righteousness, and all these things shall be added to you.* We seek first the Kingdom, and when we do, seek His righteousness with it. This is the knowing the rights you have as a citizen of the Kingdom.

So because I am born again, I am a citizen of the Kingdom, it does not matter what I did yesterday or the day before, if I am repentant, or have repented, I can stand blameless before the King and place a demand (for all these things) by virtue of the Constitution (His Word) and He must fulfill it!

Economy

There is an economic system of wealth which guarantees each citizen equal access to financial security. In a kingdom, the term common-wealth is used because the king's desire is that all his citizens share and benefit from the wealth of the kingdom. The kingdom's glory is in the prosperity and health of its citizens.

Like the other laws of the earthly realm, the economic system of this worlds kingdom is also subject to the Kingdom of God. I wrote another book called Thy Kingdom Come that is just on the economic system and overcoming the economic system of this world though Kingdom principles. At the end of this book, I will provide a link to a free digital copy for anyone who desires to read further after this section.

But here is what is important to know; the worlds economic system is set up as a chief system and governor within the kingdom of this earth. It is set up as a reciprocal to the Kingdom of God which does not work with a physical currency, but rather a system where everything is made available to you, all the time.

1 Timothy 6:10

> *For the love of money is the root of all evil: which while some coveted after, they have erred from the faith, and pierced them-selves through with many sorrows.*

The NIV says it this way:

For the love of money is a root of all kinds of evil. Some people, eager for money, have wandered from the faith and pierced themselves with many griefs.

The value people place on money in this world is beyond where it should be; in fact, a study of Like 16 reveals to us that it is a god of mammon. Jesus goes on to say in vs 13 that *"No one can serve two masters. Either you will hate the one and love the other, or you will be devoted to the one and despise the other. You cannot serve both God and money."*

Nearly 43,000 Americans commit suicide every year, making it the 10th-highest cause of death in the country. Indeed, between 1950 and 1999""a period of serious economic growth in America""""suicides among people younger than 24 increased by 137 percent. Nearly 43 million Americans experience some form of mental illness each year. Why?

Because the primary objective of money and the worlds system is owner-ship... **Mine, mine mine!** And when others have what you think you need and cannot get, the enemy makes you feel like less of a person and people become willing to sin to get what they think they need.

Listen, in the worlds system money can buy you a

House- but not a - Home

Sex - but not – Love

A Wedding – but not – a Marriage

A Vacation – but not – Peace or rest

Happiness (temporal) – but not – Joy

A Doctor – but not – Health

A Bible – but not – Understanding (revelation)

Companionship – but not – Friendship

And the list goes on and on...

There are limitations and illusions attached to this worlds economic system that is designed to become a snare to those who put it first.

In the West, our prevailing economic worldview sees people as self-interested individuals with limitless desires in a limited world, who seek to increase consumption and leisure by earning as much money as possible. We wake up and spend 40-50-60 or more hours a week chasing money and this limiting illusion and far less time seeking the Kingdom of God.

Matthew 6:33

> *But seek ye first the kingdom of God, and his righteousness; and all these things shall be added unto you.*

When you fully understand your Kingdom rights as an Ambassador of the Kingdom and your direct relationship with the King through His appointed Governor, you will understand that *the The kingdoms of this world are become the kingdoms of our Lord, and of his Christ; and he shall reign for ever and ever.* (Revelation 11:15). And because what is to come on earth already is in heaven, they are already His and under your dominion within the Kingdom!!

In other words, everything in this natural world, is subject to the supernatural; the kingdom of this world is subservient to the Kingdom of God and must come into the obedience of the King.

So then we understand that King Jesus also has unique economic policies, his own economic program.

Then there's Jesus, with:

- His parables of well-dressed lilies that neither labor nor spin, and wealthy farmers punished for saving too much.
- His commands to lend without expecting return and to invest in heavenly dwellings.
- His establishment of communities in which "no one claimed that any of their possessions was their own" (Acts 4:32).

Let me work it out, because I promise this will free you from any financially limiting thoughts and open up a new world of wisdom to you, if you get understanding on this one matter. You are about to get some life changing Kingdom understanding... I urge you to read this chapter several times if you need to in order to understand its application of principle in your life.

Luke 12-31-32 NKJV

> But seek the Kingdom of God, and all these things shall be added to you. Do not fear, little flock, _for it is your Father's good pleasure to give you the Kingdom._

Remember, in a Kingdom, a King owns everything within the kingdom.

Psalms 24:1

> ...The earth is the LORD'S, and the fulness thereof; the world, and they that dwell therein.

Who's is it? The Lords.. and where is it? Within His Kingdom.. We have access as citizens to the Kingdom, all of it. You have access right now to everything you need to get everything you want.

An article by Dr. Myles Monroe that I read puts it this way:

"The foundation of the Kingdom of God's economy is *access*. It (access) is more powerful than ownership. The foundation of the world's economy is *private ownership*.

The spirit of ownership creates many problems. Some of them are limitation, frustration, stress, contention, scarcity, lack, stealing, poverty, and sickness. That's why the child of God shouldn't model his or her thinking in the area of finances (or wealth in general) after the world's system.

When Jesus told (and still tells) you not worry (Mathew 6:25-33), He was protecting you from sicknesses and diseases. Learning to trust Him with your *whole heart* will free you from lot of ills that consume people on a daily basis.

When He becomes the Lord (or dictator) of all you have you understand that He owns it all – you are just a custodian of the things in your possession – and the **looking after** of those things is His responsibility.

Ecclesiastes 10:19 is a well-known verse of scripture. It says, *'A feast is made for laughter, and wine makes merry; but money answers everything.'* But the Bible says something interesting in the twelfth verse of the fifth chapter of the same book (Ecclesiastes 5:12). It says, *'The sleep of a labouring man is sweet, whether he eats little or much; but the* **abundance of the rich will not permit him to sleep.'**

The Kingdom of heaven's economy is not built by money – it is based on access.

Ecclesiastes 5:12-14 shows us how God sees man when he (man) hoards and stores things for himself like there's no tomorrow – it's an exercise in futility.

Now God is not against people saving or being responsible. All He's saying is 'what do you have that you did not receive?' That was the problem he had with the rich man (see Luke 12:16-21). He was not against the man being rich – it was his (the rich man) pride that put Him (God) off. The word 'I' is mentioned six times in those verses. He gloried in himself rather than in the mercy of God. He claimed ownership rather than access, and the rest is history.

It's important for you to know how the Almighty would have you do things. Ecclesiastes 5:15 shows us that man leaves with *nothing after a life of toiling*. (I have an Uncle who always said "I've never seen a brinks truck following a hearse"!)

God's way is access which comes through Lordship. Jesus never preached democracy, communism, socialism, or religion. He came with something different.

He knew that religion was not the answer – it has caused more problems than it solved. Even some of Jesus' disciples desired the destruction of their opponents in the name of religion (see Luke 9:54-56). Jesus said, 'I have not come to destroy men's lives, but to *save them*.' That's my King Jesus! He's the greatest!

A kingdom is opposite to democracy – the center of a kingdom is the king. The key to biblical economics is the Lordship of the king. I want to show you the key that freed me from lack and poverty. It is claiming *ownership of nothing while having access to all things*.

The solution to all the problems in the world is operating by the kingdom. All kingdoms have an economy called common wealth – a term used only in kingdoms. Democracies are not built for common wealth – they are for opportunists. In a true kingdom, wealth is common; though nobody owns it.

Jesus regularly talked about the Kingdom of God (see Matthew 3:2; 4:17, 22; 5:3; 6:33, and Luke 4:43). In Matthew 6:9, Jesus said to pray,

'**Our** (not my) Father...' In other words, come to the father for common wealth – not just wealth for yourself. Jesus didn't ask us to pray to go to heaven; He asked us to pray for heaven to come to earth (see Matthew 6:10).

The concept of Lordship is the key to the Kingdom of God's economy. Getting this truth into your spirit and consistently practicing it will get lack out your life forever. Jesus didn't preach an economy of personal pursuit; but one of common wealth.

The Key to a kingdom is the King, and the glory of the kingdom is territory – unlike a democracy. The word *owner* is 'Adonai' in Greek. It means **Lord** or *possessor*. In true kingdoms there is no private owner-ship. You own nothing – but have access to everything. The most common word in the Bible is **Lord** – maybe that why it has lost its true meaning today.

If a person claims ownership to anything, they attract God's judgment. If a person claims ownership to anything, they attract God's judgment. God owns everything – man is just a custodian. God owns everything – man is just a custodian. (you are not seeing double!) Genesis 1 begins with the statement, 'In the beginning God created the heaven (500 million galaxies) and the earth.' That's not a suggestion, but a statement of fact! In Exodus 6, God manifested Himself to Moses in a way that He didn't when He was with Abraham. He revealed Himself to Abraham as God Almighty (the supplier of his needs), but He revealed Himself to Moses as Jehovah (the one who is faithful to fulfill His promises and covenants). Even Pilate couldn't do anything to Jesus without the permission of heaven – he was a tool in God's hands.

Who is the Lord? The Hebrew word 'Yahweh' is translated Lord – it is used for Lordship. There's no private ownership in Kingdoms. The two most dangerous concepts in the kingdom are *independence* and *own-ership*.

Lordship is the key to economic success.

In a kingdom the citizens are stewards – they use what is given to them for a while, until the king asks for it. I believe you can make this a turn-around year for you because you will function with an understanding of the Lordship of God's like you never have before.

Jesus demonstrated Lordship by asking His disciples to go and get the donkey for His use (Matthew 21) – remember? *The Master has use of it!* Only He could do that. That's Lordship! It was His – the person they (His disciples) took it from was just the custodian! God's owns everything – you have access to it all!

Someone may be holding stuff that God has reserved for you – it's about to come into your hands because it's not theirs. Never be jealous about anybody because God owns everything".

Luke 12-31-32 NKJV

> But seek the Kingdom of God, and all these things shall be added to you. Do not fear, little flock, *for it is your Father's good pleasure to give you the Kingdom.*

Here is the "Anthony Reinglas" translation of this scripture and Mathew 6:33 as a cross reference:

> Pursue the Kingdom, seek after the culture of the Kingdom, seek the King, know your rights as a Kingdom citizen and understand your authority and then everything that you need in life will be given to you because it is already yours in the Kingdom where the King takes pleasure in giving it to you!

Kingdom Culture

From the time of the introduction of the Kingdom by Jesus Christ, it was apparent that its structure was exactly opposite to the structure of the kingdoms of this world. Residency in the Kingdom of God requires a new lifestyle governed by the laws of the Kingdom of God.

Your life in the spiritual Kingdom affects the quality of life in the visible world. The lifestyle of the Kingdom is exactly opposite of the lifestyle of the kingdoms of the world. It is different in both structure and principles. In the natural world, "culture" is the behavior patterns which govern life in a given society. When you enter the Kingdom of God it is like immigrating to a new country. **You must learn a different culture.**

We have the culture of this world so engrained in us that when we come into the Kingdom of God, our natural minds reject the laws, principles and keys of the Kingdom and it takes a severe reprograming to fully comprehend and actually walk in it... Somewhat like the move *The Matrix*, where the star had to get his self-imposed limitations out of his head before he can unlock his full potential. We can compare it to the culture shock of going into another unknown culture.

Then the social cultural aspect of a kingdom is the environment created by the life and manners of the king and his citizens. This is the cultural aspect that separates and distinguishes the kingdom from all others around it. It is the culture that expresses the nature of the king, through the lifestyle of his citizens. This distinction in kingdom culture is evident in the words of the Lord Jesus, when He said in the book of

Matthew 5:21-22

> *You have heard that our ancestors were told, 'You must not murder. If you commit murder, you are subject to judgment.' But I say, if you are even angry with someone, you are subject*

to judgment! If you call someone an idiot, you are in danger of being brought before the court. And if you curse someone, you are in danger of the fires of hell.

and again in Matthew 20:25-28

But Jesus called them together and said, "You know that the rulers in this world lord it over their people, and officials flaunt their authority over those under them. But among you it will be different. Whoever wants to be a leader among you must be your servant, and whoever wants to be first among you must become your slave. For even the Son of Man came not to be served but to serve others and to give His life as a ransom for many."

The Kingdom social culture should be evident in our daily activities and encounters. If we are part of His Kingdom, we will reflect the culture of our King! When you live in the Kingdom and by the Kingdom culture, you take on the personality of the Kingdom itself and your deeds and actions should reflect the Kingdom on all you do. And by this nature, you seek to expand the Kingdom of God continually, Just as Jesus did, you preach and teach the Kingdom and go about doing good, healing all those oppressed of the devil, because the King is with you!

Religion is one of the biggest adversaries to Kingdom Culture that there is, so I will dedicate the next chapter to it.

Another vital part of the culture is atmosphere.

Ever walk in a room where people were arguing and even though it's quiet, you can sense fighting in the atmosphere? Ever go to a movie where you felt the atmosphere shift to one that was created in the movie? I remember as a kid we would watch Bruce Lee Kung Fu movies and afterwards we would be imitating the Asian martial artist as if we were him! What about when you play worship or praise music for a sustained period of time? You can sense the atmosphere of praise.

Certain things produce atmosphere.. What you can see, taste, hear and sense with your natural senses can affect the spiritual atmosphere. This is why Praise stills the avenger (psalm 8:2).. it creates a Kingdom atmosphere and the enemy is not permitted in the Kingdom!

We can study out and find that atmosphere can produce climates that produce strongholds (good or bad), that produce culture. This is why it is important to sustain an atmosphere of praise and worship in your heart and home. You will attract what is dominant because you create the atmosphere around you; so make sure you always entertain a Kingdom atmosphere.

> **Tidbit:** Music is the only thing that affects all three parts of your soul; the lyrics affect your mind, the beat affects your will and the melody affects your emotions. Lucifer was the chief musician and worship leader in heaven before he was cast down as lighting to the earth. He knows how to create and dominate atmosphere better than most of us. Secular music is made with one purpose and one purpose only and that is to bring your soul as far from the Kingdom atmosphere as possible until a stronghold is created.

Let the culture of the Kingdom be in you so much that the world bends to the very atmosphere around you. This is one way we exercise dominion and subdue the earth.

Language

Every Kingdom has either its own language, dialect or principle paths of communication. The Kingdom of God is no different. In our previous understanding about words and atmospheres this is important, because the language of the Kingdom invokes an atmosphere of the Kingdom, which brings manifest the results and benefits of the Kingdom!

Let's go back to the garden.

When God created man as a reflection of Himself and put him in the garden to have dominion and expand it, there was no distance between God and man, because there was no difference (their minds and spirits were aligned). God would walk with Adam and converse with him in the garden... What a wonderful picture that paints! During this time it would stand to reason, that both God and Adam spoke the same language. Some say it was, and is, the language of angels, but all it was is the language of the Kingdom.

This is my conjecture, and it would stand to reason that when Adam sinned, he had to depart from the garden, then we know that separation came; and so, because he was no longer in the Kingdom, he could no longer speak or understand the language of the Kingdom. The original language of the kingdom which allowed man to have direct access to God and unrestricted communication had been removed and a distance was placed between God and man.

Man communicated through whatever language was established after the fall and remained united with each other, and was able to converse and reason with each other, but not with God. Then something else would happen...

One of the biggest causes of separation among the people of the world is language. When God intended mankind to spread across the face of the Earth, man disobeyed and formed a religious system in unison against God's instructions. God's intervention was a confounding of the languages to stop this false religion.

Genesis 11:9

Therefore is the name of it called Babel; because the LORD did there confound the language of all the earth: and from thence did the LORD scatter them abroad upon the face of all the earth.

From the separation of the people, God chose one man and one nation to work through. Israel was given the privilege of God's words and blessings if they obeyed. But when Israel broke God's law the punishment was to be overtaken by people of languages they neither knew nor understood.

Jeremiah 5:15

Lo, I will bring a nation upon you from far, O house of Israel, saith the LORD: it is a mighty nation, it is an ancient nation, a nation whose language thou knowest not, neither understandest what they say.

It is a horrible situation not to speak the language of your rulers. You are considered second-class residents and outcasts. Stammering tongues and other languages were not beneficial, as some would describe today. It was utter confusion! It was used as a punishment by God.

Despite their rebellion God would remember the promise he made to make Israel a mighty nation. In the coming kingdom to Jerusalem they would once again have a pure language.

Isaiah 19:18

In that day shall five cities in the land of Egypt speak the language of Canaan, and swear to the LORD of hosts; one shall be called, The city of destruction.

Zeph 3:9

> *For then will I turn to the people a pure language, that they may all call upon the name of the LORD, to serve him with one consent.*

At the fulfillment of these prophecies God would reunite the world under the Messiah, our King. One means of doing this would be the restoration of the language of the Kingdom. It is not surprising when we read about the twelve apostles preaching prophetic fulfillment that they supernaturally speak in the languages of the nations.

Acts 2:4,6

> *They were all filled with the Holy Ghost, and began to speak with other tongues, as the Spirit gave them utterance....Now when this was noised abroad, the multitude came together, and were confounded, because that every man heard them speak in his own language.*

This is the exact opposite of the confounding at Babel, it was a confounding that there was no longer a language barrier! What an amazing divine removal of the language problem.

The tongue talking at Pentecost was not a greater diversifying of the languages, but a unifying of the languages. It allowed everyone who heard the apostles to understand what they were preaching. It was also a sign that their message was true: the kingdom was coming. The prophesied kingdom to Israel could not come without this one language restitution.

Here is what Jesus says we can expect when we step into the Kingdom:

Mark 16:17

> *And these signs shall follow them that believe; In my name shall they cast out devils; they shall speak with new tongues...*

Once again, through the restoration that our Lord Jesus brought, there is also a restoration of the language and open communication between man and God. Because the Governor, the Holy Spirit dwells in you, He becomes your interpreter. Because the Holy Spirit is searching your spirit and knows all things, He knows the perfect prayer to pray on your behalf, but it is still up to you to speak it. The restoration of this prayer language is one of the most powerful tools in the Kingdom you can have because it is how we communicate, in our perfected language, in your most holy faith, to the King Himself!

1 Corinthians 14:2

> *For he that speaketh in an unknown tongue speaketh not unto men, but unto God: for no man understandeth him; howbeit in the spirit he speaketh mysteries.*

Praying in tongues is a supernatural language that cannot be studied, learned, or written in any college or university because it is not a natural language and one of the Kingdom. Whenever you speak in tongues, you are speaking to God's ears without interference. It is the hidden wisdom of God that is made manifest though you. Need wisdom? Pray in tongues!

The devil cannot understand you; neither can he interfere with or intercept your communication with your Father. It is an untainted conversation between you and the King that no one can interfere with. In fact, it is foolishness to them who do not believe. Yet, it is a supernatural language that breaks the laws of time and physics, because in the Kingdom, in the spirit, there is no time and there are no physical limitations. So you can be praying for 10 different things at the same time, and some may have already happened while others, not quite yet! Can you wrap your mind around what I just said? Your prayer language can reach across time and space and put angels in motion and affect the atmosphere anywhere in our realm!

Acts 2:4

> *And everyone present was filled with the Holy Spirit and began speaking in other languages, as the Holy Spirit gave them this ability.*

When you are baptized in the Holy Spirit, you receive a gift from God: The ability to speak the language of the Kingdom, which is the gift of speaking (or praying) in tongues. It is a powerful gift that every believer should desire. In fact, here are five benefits to praying in tongues:

1. Praying in Tongues Allows You to Speak Directly to God

"For if you have the ability to speak in tongues, you will be talking only to God, since people won't be able to understand you. You will be speaking by the power of the Spirit, but it will all be mysterious." –1 Corinthians 14:2

When you pray in tongues, you are praying God's will, directly to Him. It allows your mind to get out of the way so your spirit can commune with the Father.

1. Praying in Tongues Keeps You in Tune With the Holy Spirit

"And everyone present was filled with the Holy Spirit and began speaking in other languages, as the Holy Spirit gave them this ability." –Acts 2:4

Tongues is a gift from God. It allows you to pray the will of God by the empowering of the Holy Spirit. When you pray in tongues, you are yielding to the Holy Spirit who dwells in you. Then you are allowing that same Spirit to pray through you, so you are in tune with Him.

1. Praying in Tongues Strengthens Your Spirit

"A person who speaks in tongues is strengthened personally, but one who speaks a word of prophecy strengthens the entire church." –1 Corinthians 14:4

Praying in tongues builds you up spiritually and helps you to live a Spirit-led life.

1. **Praying in Tongues Allows You to Pray Even When You Don't Know What to Pray**

"And the Holy Spirit helps us in our weakness. For example, we don't know what God wants us to pray for. But the Holy Spirit prays for us with groanings that cannot be expressed in words." –Romans 8:26

Even when you don't know how or what to pray, you can still pray...in tongues. You can trust your spirit to pray the perfect will of God, regardless of the situation.

1. **Praying in Tongues Is a Weapon Against the Work of the Enemy**

"And then he told them, 'Go into all the world and preach the Good News to everyone. Anyone who believes and is baptized will be saved.... These miraculous signs will accompany those who believe: They will cast out demons in my name, and they will speak in new languages.... They will be able to place their hands on the sick, and they will be healed.'" –Mark 16:15-18

Jesus proclaimed several things that would happen to those who followed Him and continued His work. Speaking in tongues is one of those gifts, and it allows Jesus' followers to stand against the work of the enemy.

Praying in tongues is a gift that's available to every believer. It allows you to pray God's will to Him. It keeps you in tune with the Holy Spirit and strengthens your spirit as you stand against the work of the devil. Don't discount this powerful gift from God. Desire it. Embrace it and relish the strength it adds to your spiritual life.

If praying in tongues hasn't been a regular part of your fellowship with God, you're missing out! There is so much power found in praying in tongues, not to mention answers to any question you have, access to inside information, and a spiritual strengthening like no other.

Acts 2:4

> *And they were all filled with the Holy Spirit and began to speak with other tongues, as the Spirit gave them utterance*

1 Corinthians 14:4

He who speaks in a tongue edifies himself.

Romans 8:26

> *Likewise the Spirit also helps in our weaknesses. For we do not know what we should pray for as we ought, but the Spirit Himself makes intercession for us with groanings which cannot be uttered.*

Romans 8:27 *(NIV)*

The Spirit intercedes for God's people in accordance with the will of God.

1 Corinthians 14:2 *(AMPC)*

> *For one who speaks in an [unknown] tongue speaks not to men but to God, for no one understands or catches his meaning, because in the [Holy] Spirit he utters secret truths and hidden things [not obvious to the understanding].*

Jude 20

> But you, beloved, building yourselves up on your most holy faith, praying in the Holy Spirit.

1 Corinthians 14:14

For if I pray in an unknown tongue, my spirit prayeth, but my understanding is unfruitful.

1 Corinthians 14:18

I thank my God, I speak with tongues more than ye all

John 16:13

> *However, when He, the Spirit of truth, has come, He will guide you into all truth; for He will not speak on His own authority, but whatever He hears He will speak; and He will tell you things to come.*

When you take the time to study the Word (The Constitution) and its emphasis on the power of praying in tongues (The language of the Kingdom), you'll build your faith to move into times of this special fellowship with the Lord. You are never alone, and you are never without answers.. You will find the hidden wisdom and answers as well as having prayers answered speedily and find that moving mountains and parting waters is not as hard as your natural mind would make you think!

I challenge you to speak to the King for at least 30 minutes every day in His language. It will change your life for the better, and without a doubt give you results that are out of this world!

The Army

We know very well that *The thief comes only to steal, kill, and destroy* (John 10:10); and by 2 Corinthians 10:4, we know that *the weapons of our warfare are not carnal, but mighty through God to the pulling down of strong holds..* So as Christians and Kingdom Citizens, we must be aware of the fact that we are involved in warfare with the devil. This warfare is not a social event that we can decline. Although Satan's primary weapons are deception of our mind and sickness of our body and his main strategy is to deceive us so that we do not realize that we have an enemy that is attacking us. He tries to hide you from understanding your true power and authority of your citizen rights of the Kingdom of God. But God has given us every weapon that we need to defeat the devil, to be victorious through Jesus Christ.

I hear many say, and we even sing songs that we are Gods Army. That's simply not true. First, God does not need protection, secondly, if He did, it certainly would not be us protecting Him or His Kingdom! Our fight is with the enemy between our two ears and the battlefield is the mind. Once you get a true Kingdom understanding, you will not need to fight!

The Kingdom Army is the Kings system of securing its territory and protecting its citizens. It is important to understand that in a kingdom the citizens do not fight, but enjoy the protection of the army. This is why, in the Kingdom of God, the angels are called the host of heaven. The word host means army and identifies the angels as the so-called military component of the Kingdom of Heaven.

This Kingdom concept presents a challenge to our religious thinking of the church as an army. A careful study of the biblical constitution of the

Word will show that the church, as Jesus established it, is not identified as an army but rather a citizenship, a family of sons and daughters, and a nation.

Matthew 26:52-53

> *"Put away your sword," Jesus told him. "Those who use the sword will die by the sword. Don't you realize that I could ask My Father for thousands of angels to protect us, and He would send them instantly?*

Psalm 78:49

> *He loosed on them His fierce anger—all His fury, rage, and hostility. He dispatched against them a band of destroying angels.*

Psalm 103:20-21

> *Praise the Lord, you angels, you mighty ones who carry out His plans, listening for each of His commands. Yes, praise the Lord, you armies of angels who serve Him and do His will!*

Matthew 13:40-42

> *Just as the weeds are sorted out and burned in the fire, so it will be at the end of the world. The Son of Man will send His angels, and they will remove from His Kingdom everything that causes sin and all who do evil. And the angels will throw them into the fiery furnace, where there will be weeping and gnashing of teeth.*

Psalm 91:11-12 (NKJV)

For He shall give His angels charge over you, to keep you in all your ways.

In their hands they shall bear you up.

When you are abiding in Gods Kingdom and obeying His Constitution, you have the right to utilize the army of the ministry of angels God has provided. It's part of your citizenship package!

He provided these powerful beings to aid you on the earth, to bless you, and to minister to you.

If you haven't been tapping into this powerful, supernatural resource, begin today with these five ways to put your angels to work.

These *5 Ways To Put Your Angels To Work* are from an article by Gloria Copeland that I found to be inspiring:

1. Speak the Word.

When you find yourself in a situation—one of possible physical danger, one where you need deliverance, or one where you require material or financial help—speak the Word only. And do so in faith. This allows your angels to minister to you on your behalf—to work for you, to intervene. When you speak against the Word of God, their hands are tied—they can't move an inch to help you.

Gloria Copeland shares how she does this: "Whatever happens in my life—if I'm in danger—I don't panic. I stay calm, and I start reciting Psalm 91. I say, 'God is my refuge, God is my deliverance.' It has saved my life before."

Years ago, when she and Kenneth were getting ready to travel to South Africa, many people encouraged them to take security with them because it was volatile there at the time. Gloria responded, "I don't go anywhere without security. Glory to God. Every time I go to the grocery store, I have security. The Bible says angels encamp around those who fear Him" (Psalm 34:7).

2. Command your angels.

Can you really do this? In short, yes. Keep in mind, you aren't commanding them in the same way you are commanding and rebuking the devil. You are releasing them to do the work they've been assigned to perform on your behalf.

You have been given the authority of Jesus Christ, as an heir, and you can command your angels to move on your behalf to carry out the Word (Psalm 103:20). Kenneth Copeland advises saying something like this: "In the Name of Jesus, ministering spirits, I assign you according to Hebrews 1:13-14 to see to it that I have protection in this car, in this airplane, in this building. I claim this right as an heir to salvation."

3. Pray for angels.

When you ask God to deploy your angels, He will do so. Jesus said God would have sent 12 legions of angels to His rescue had He asked for them. Prayer will release angels on your behalf (Matthew 26:51-53). Every time you leave your house, ask that angels protect you in every vehicle you ride in, every building you walk in, and every situation.

4. Call on the Name of Jesus.

The Name of Jesus catches the attention of God's angels. They will respond to the Name above all names and come to your rescue (Hebrews 1:6). The Name of Jesus is powerful! When you're in a situation where you need help, call on His Name. He'll send help your way!

5. Thank God for His help.

When you trust and believe that God will send His angels to help you (Psalm 91:11), you are receiving their intervention by faith. Thank Him and praise Him because He has given His angels charge over you. Thank Him for providing you with an entire army to enforce what is rightfully yours.

Isn't it good to know you don't have to depend on your own abilities for protection and deliverance? So you fight your good fight by renewing your mind to the Word of God; which is understanding the Constitution and your rights, so that you can rule and have the dominion you are meant to, and let Gods army watch your back as you do!

Get your angels involved in your life. God's will is for you to enjoy everything He provided through Jesus on the cross, and He's provided all the help you'll ever need!

Closing Tidbit: When you pray in tongues, the language of the Kingdom, you are engaging the Governor (the Holy Spirit) and speaking directly to the King who is then employing the Army of the Kingdom to minister and move on your behalf and carry out your petition! The activity going on in the invisible realm of the Kingdom is more real and active and dominant than any situation, circumstance or state of affairs on this earth! Remember.. you are in it, but not of it!

IV

Religious Mindsets

As we read and now understand, every Kingdom has a culture. Most cultures do not realize that they are culturized, or to what extent they are actually programmed until you go to another culture and see how different it really is in that culture... This is commonly known as culture shock.

So we learn in our culture that the educational system, economic system, values, healthcare, social, political and even religious systems have to be a certain way because that's the way it's always been and that's what we know to be true and correct. But nobody questions these things.. we just go on, living our lives in our own virtual petri dishes happy, as so long as the other cultures from the other dishes do not spill over into ours and upsets our way of thinking and doing things.

I know the reality of that may hurt, but if you take a minute to ponder the truth of it, you will realize that the world is made up of millions of different cultures and then sub cultures and even as granular as different family cultures; and each one is unique in itself.

I grew up in Brooklyn NY, in an Italian-American area.. As a kid, all I knew was spaghetti on Sunday, everyone went to Catholic Church, and it was a tight knit neighborhood where everyone knew everyone and there was virtually no crime because the social club on the corner made sure to keep it clean. We used to be able to go out and play until 11pm and our parents didn't have to worry about us... And if I got out of line, someone else's dad would spank my rear! Sure, go home and tell dad... he'd spank me again for whatever it was I did to deserve it! I just thought that this is how it was all over and in other neighborhoods. This was the early culture I was exposed to and grew up in... Until I was old enough to go to other areas and find out that after 8pm, it's not safe to be on the street, I thought the whole world was like my myopic Catholic Italian sub culture of Brooklyn, NY! AS we grow up we become more exposed to other cultures and we realize that ours was most comfortable for us, and soon, we migrate back to wence we came. Most people remain in the religions they grow up in, eat the same foods they grew up on and never even move out of the same neighborhoods they were raised in because the reality is, it because a stronghold in us. It is a religious spirit at the root.

So let me elaborate on an earlier thought to take it a bit further.

I said that if you sustain an atmosphere long enough, it changes the climate, and if you sustain the climate long enough it becomes a stronghold and changes the culture. Well here's how the spirit world works... All spirit needs a body to seek expression (this is how things are manifest from the spirit).

Good or bad, every spirit needs a body to express anything in this physical world. So the enemy comes at you with a thought that says *hit that guy that just cut you off*, and the Holy Spirit in you is saying *Forgive him and pray for him because he's having a bad day*.. Which thought you entertain will be the most dominant and will control your atmosphere as you dwell on it... OOPS, now you're getting angry because you took the wrong thought maybe start cussing a bit, before you know it, you're in road rage and showing that driver who's boss! Do you see the atmosphere shifting over you? Do you feel it? Well, if you consistently entertain this type of atmosphere, sooner or later you will find that you just become one mean, nasty driver who is only out for himself and eventually it will lead to some form of loss or destruction and the enemy had his way because he shifted the atmosphere with a thought.

This works in the inverse also of course, which is why we always want to take Kingdom sustaining thoughts:

Phil 4:8

> *Finally, brethren, whatsoever things are true, whatsoever things are honest, whatsoever things are just, whatsoever things are pure, whatsoever things are lovely, whatsoever things are of good report; if there be any virtue, and if there be any praise, think on these things.*

Thoughts become strongholds and strongholds will always limit your understanding of anything that opposes it. So when the religious stronghold is challenged with the truth of the Gospel of the Kingdom, it is hard to break. This book and its contents are a perfected example. This is how we are supposed to live, solely in the Kingdom, having dominion and subduing the earth while expanding and multiplying what the King gave us... but just look at our lives how far from it we've gone. And not only gone, but deemed normal and I some cases even healthy, God willing this book is making an impact and breaking the religious mindset and stronghold of this earthly kingdom in you and your thinking.

We come into the Kingdom of God with preconceived notions, ideologies and mindsets from the dominant culture that we grew up in, or spent the majority of our lives building ourselves within and upon. lives and building upon the realities that we've created for ourselves in our own minds; and this becomes our standard.

The devil messed up the church right from the beginning by turning it into a religion... and when people are thinking religion, they never get into relationship.

Jesus said when he healed a little boy by the Spirit of God, "*If I healed him by the Spirit of God then the kingdom of God has come upon you...* " What that means is that the healing that came, is only a result of the Kingdom

When you worry, that's a sign that you are religious... It means you don't understand concepts of Kingdom... But don't worry , by the time you are done with this book, you will be casting out devils, speaking to mountains and living in a way that will astound all that know you!

So this apparent dichotomy of two opposing kingdoms, is a minute by minute choice to press into the Kingdom (*Luke 16:16*) until it becomes your everyday reality more so than your existing earthly routine and realm is now.

Let this mind be in you which was also in Christ Jesus

What was the mind of the King Jesus? The Kingdom!

V

Kingdom of the World vs Kingdom of God

The Kingdom of God as we have already learned is vastly different from the kingdom of this world; but as we have also learned, that is not how God created it to be.

A definition of a kingdom is: A kingdom is the governing influence of a king over a territory, impacting that territory with his will, his purpose, and his intent, producing a culture and a moral standard for his citizens.

Notice...these benefits belong only to his citizens. Citizenship matters greatly. An individual's welfare depends on it. When man fell, the second kingdom was exposed to him and he became subordinate to it by virtue of his rebellion to Gods rule. You may say it was only one law that Adam broke, and that's true.. But realize that God only had one law then.. Do not eat from that tree.

The understanding of kingdom rulership is hard for us to apprehend in its fullest in America because we were born in and grew up in a Democratic Republic where the people rule (or are supposed to) as opposed to a king; a place where each person strives for and works to obtain his own piece of the pie. But as we are revealing and restating throughout this book (so you engrain the understanding in your mind), a kingdom works much different.

America was once under the rule of a king. We were founded and chartered under Great Brittan. Great Brittan then was a kingdom and operated in all manners of a kingdom; however, the king then has committed many atrocities against the settlers in our American Colony, and succession against a tyrannous government was necessary at that time.

I did a little research and made a simple but profound (to me) revelation concerning our roots that may be a contributing factor to the dominant stronghold and culture in America of rebellion against authority.

America is not founded on the declaration of Independence and Constitution... Those documents were founded on the culture of the people that were already in America at the time of their writings... and they were a reflection and a result of who we had already become and chose to become as a nation to be united.

A little history lesson:

Samuel de Champlain Voyages to America in 1604 and sets up the first Virginia Colony in 1606

Three ships, the Godspeed, the Discovery, and the Constance all sailed into Chesapeake Bay near Cape Henry Virginia.

John Smith was the captain of the voyage and the first thing they did upon coming to dry land was to erect a cross on dry land to worship and give thanks. They then created the first Charter, or official Document ever on file with regard to the formation of America. It was known as the First Charter of Virginia.. it reads:

1. *We, greatly commending and graciously accepting of their desires to the furtherance of so noble a work which may, by the providence of Almighty God, hereafter tend to the glory of His Divine Majesty in propagating of Christian religion to such people as yet live in*

darkness and miserable ignorance of the true knowledge and wor-ship of God...

The charter contains only one statement of purpose, a religious mission: "propagating of Christian religion".

The U.S. declaration of independence from the United Kingdom in 1776 was a momentous event, but why did the 13 colonies declare independence? Fortunately, a group of colonial representatives wrote down all of the reasons why in one document: the appropriately named Declaration of Independence.

In Congress, July 4, 1776.

The unanimous Declaration of the thirteen united States of America,

When in the Course of human events, it becomes necessary for one people to dissolve the political bands which have connected them with another, and to assume among the powers of the earth, the separate and equal station to which the Laws of Nature and of Nature's God entitle them, a decent respect to the opinions of mankind requires that they should declare the causes which impel them to the separation.

We hold these truths to be self-evident, that all men are created equal, that they are endowed by their Creator with certain unalienable Rights, that among these are Life, Liberty and the pursuit of Happiness.--That to secure these rights, Governments are instituted among Men, deriving their just powers from the consent of the governed, --That whenever any Form of Government becomes destructive of these ends, it is the Right of the People to alter or to abolish it, and to institute new Government, laying its foundation on such principles and organizing its powers in such form, as to them shall seem most likely to effect their Safety and Happiness.....

Although we were under rule of a kingship, his rule was not one that the American settlers desired or wanted because they felt that the king was not representing their interest adequately. When I look closer at this, I see a change of intent. The original intent was to propagate the Christian religion to people in darkness and 170 years later it was to pursue life, liberty and happiness. Today, another 246 years later America is still pursuing freedom and happiness, only without any values because there is no headship or authority or moral rule. Freedom without authority is the definition of anarchy. (and we wonder why after 250 years of religious freedom in America we are in the failed condition we are in.)

So while it is for these reasons that our understanding of a kingdom needs to be refined more so in America than someone of another country where they may already have this understanding, I cannot state it enough that a kingdom is the governing influence of a king over a territory, impacting that territory with his will, his purpose, and his intent, producing a culture and a moral standard for his citizens. In other words, the kingdom, the king, the territory, the people and everything inside it belong to the king and are a direct expression of the king himself. Such as it is with the Kingdom of God and all of its colonies or providences.

The kingdom of this world or earth is a colony of the Kingdom of Heaven and God placed man in the colony as an ambassador of His Kingdom and empowered him with all the authority and power of the King Himself to subdue the earth, have dominion and to multiply everything that was within the Kingdom (then the garden of Eden) throughout the rest of the earth until the entire earth was filed with His glory.

Habakkuk 2:14

> *the earth will be filled with the knowledge of the glory of the Lord,*
> *as the waters cover the sea*

The glory of a king is his territory, his entire domain.

You were made in the image of God, the King. To be in the image of God means to reflect him and represent him, and reflecting God is the same thing as glorifying God.

So now while we live in the kingdom of this world, it is our task as citizens of the Kingdom of God to pick up the task of glorifying the King and expanding the Kingdom here on earth with the knowledge of the glory of the Lord, and the good news of the Kingdom proclaimed and demonstrated in the whole world as a testimony to all nations, and then the end will come.

It's similar to a dual citizenship, that we will discuss more about later, but you should know now that although you reside in America, Canada, New Zealand or anywhere on this earth, your country and citizenship of origin is of the Kingdom of God.

Jesus taught us to pray *"Thy Kingdom come, Thy will be done; on* (this kingdom of) *earth as it is in* (the Kingdom of) *heaven...* Two Kingdoms, one mandate. Why would He tell you to pray this, if it were not possible?

It is your task as a Kingdom citizen and Ambassador to use your authority and power of citizenship of the Kingdom to expand the Kings will on this earthly kingdom as it already is done in heaven.

We know that this is no easy task in the natural and that irrespective of your dedication to the Lord and the Kingdom, this rivalry of kingdoms will continue

Mathew 24:

> *⁷ For nation shall rise against nation, and kingdom against kingdom: and there shall be famines, and pestilences, and earthquakes, in divers places.*

> *¹⁴ And this gospel of the kingdom shall be preached in all the world for a witness unto all nations; and then shall the end come.*

And then we see in the end when the seventh trumpet sounds in:

Revelation 11:15

> *And the seventh angel sounded; and there were great voices in heaven, saying, The kingdoms of this world are become the kingdoms of our Lord, and of his Christ; and he shall reign for ever and ever.*

Until then, know that you are originated in the Kingdom of Heaven and are to rule and reign in the kingdom of this world. With a definitive resolve to the Kingdom. In other words either you are a citizen or not. Many "Christians" today are merely visitors of the Kingdom or resident aliens at best, but very few actually find the true citizenship of the Kingdom. Sadly it is because most are held up in religion or they simply love the kingdom of this world more. Now there is a hard truth here, and it does not negate the Grace, Love and the finished works of Jesus Christ on the cross in any way, but either you are a citizen, or you are not, there is no in between.

Matthew 6:24

> *No one can serve two masters. For either he will hate the one and love the other, or else he will hold to the one and despise the other."*

The word 'master' here may also be interpreted as 'lord'. Jesus is saying, if you do not serve the Lord your King, if you do not *"love the Lord your God with all your heart, and with all your soul, and with all your mind"* (**Matthew 22:37**) then you are in rebellion and belong to the enemy. What happens to the enemy of God? Jesus tells us:

Matthew 25:41

> *Depart from Me, you cursed, into everlasting fire prepared for the Devil and his angels*

This means that we are to serve God in every possible way. We cannot have split loyalty; split loyalty is totally unacceptable. We cannot pick and choose the works we do, they are assigned to us. We cannot pick and choose the verses from the Bible (ordinances of the Constitution) as to which we will accept or reject.

Matthew 13:37-38

> [37] He answered and said unto them, He that soweth the good seed is the Son of man;

> [38] The field is the world; the good seed are the children of the kingdom; but the tares are the children of the wicked one;

Now does this mean that if you do not have the full revelation of the Kingdom of God that you will not go to heaven? Certainly not! But unless a man is born again, he cannot see, understand or comprehend the Kingdom of God (John 3:3). It's a matter of a deeper revelation of your purpose here on earth which is not to just accept Jesus as your Lord and Savior, live as a good person and get to heaven; but to fulfill your purpose you must take on the original and existing purpose of man which is to have dominion over the earth, subdue it and multiply all that is within the Kingdom throughout the earth. Period.

One Visible, One Invisible

The kingdom of God is an invisible Kingdom, but it is more real than the visible one we hold our temporary residence in. Let me walk this through in scripture:

Hebrews 11:3

> *Through faith we understand that the worlds were framed by the word of God, so that things which are seen were not made of things which do appear.*

Hebrews 11:1

> *Now faith is the substance of things hoped for, the evidence of things **not seen**.*

In other words, everything that you see, hear, smell and touch are originated in the unseen world.

Colossians 1:16

> *For by him were all things created, that are in heaven, and that are in earth, visible and invisible, whether they be thrones, or dominions, or principalities, or powers: all things were created by him, and for him:*

We can understand that the things in the kingdom of this earth are seen (for the most part- some are intangible), and the things that are in the Kingdom of God are unseen to our natural senses, but most certainly exist and are more real than what we do see because what we do see, was made from what we do not.

There are several ways that "things" go from the unseen world to the seen world, from the Kingdom of God, to the kingdom of this world.

One of the realms of the kingdom of this world is the kingdom of darkness; this is where Satan operates. As a Citizen and Ambassador of the Kingdom of God, you have full authority over all these other kingdoms.

Ephesians 6:12

> *For we wrestle not against flesh and blood, but against principalities, against powers, against the rulers of the darkness of this world, against spiritual wickedness in high places.*

But Here is what your King says to its citizens (you and I):

Luke 10:19

> *Behold, I give unto you power to tread on serpents and scorpions, and over all the power of the enemy: and nothing shall by any means hurt you.*

It is because you are a citizen of the Kingdom that you can tread on serpents and scorpions, and over all the power of the enemy: and nothing shall by any means hurt you. In Acts 27 Paul is shipwrecked and gets bit by a snake, what did he do? He shook it off because he understood his rights as a Kingdom citizen. Paul understood Kingdom dominion even to the point of utilizing the wisdom here on earth when he is being whipped by his captives, Paul exclaims that he is a Citizen of Rome and they immediately stopped beating him and begged for his forgiveness!

This is how your Kingdom authority works! As a citizen, not only do you have dominion over all the earth, the fouls of the air and living creatures in the sea and everything you can see, but all forces of darkness are subject to you as well! You are a citizen of the Most High God, the Lord of Lords and King of Kings!

Luke 10:20

> *Notwithstanding in this rejoice not, that the spirits are subject unto you; but rather rejoice, because your names are written in heaven.*

The best part of it all is not that you have this power or dominion to command the spirits and subdue the earth, this is something that is as of right, simply because you are an Ambassador and Kingdom Citizen. Jesus said here in Luke to not rejoice over the fact that spirits obey you, but rather rejoice because you are a citizen of Heaven!

VI

Kingdom Citizenship

Let's talk more and get into what it means to be a citizen. Most organized groups within societies, including religions, function on the basis of membership. However, countries, nations, kingdoms—and their colonies—are different, because they function on the basis of citizenship. This is an important distinction to make, because otherwise you might assume that being part of a colony relegates you to some kind of second-class citizenship that is more like membership in a club.

You need to know that you are a full citizen of whatever nation claims your territory as a colony. This applies even to Heaven and Earth. Heaven is the territory of the King called God, although it remains largely invisible to human eyes. Heaven is God's country, if you want to call it that. Heaven is an actual place. Sometimes people who have visited it give us a glimpse of what it is like, and they report amazing experiences.

Heaven is God's headquarters. His throne is there. (The word "throne" does not mean just a fancy chair. It means a "seat of power" or citadel.)

You will hear two terms used interchangeably: the Kingdom of God and the Kingdom of Heaven. They both mean the same thing except that the first one is referring to the One who owns the Kingdom and the other is referring to the territory.

That is where we get some of our descriptive terms for God.

People call Him the King of glory,

the King of Creation,

the King of the Universe.

He is the King of everything seen as well as everything unseen.

He owns it all and He rules it from within

His original territory, Heaven.

Often, those of us who dwell on the planet called Earth fail to understand the setup. We see the physical planet all around us, and we find it to be delightful and fearful at the same time. We may recognize the existence of a world outside of our immediate experience, but we do not understand its importance. We recognize our citizenship in some nation, but we do not realize that all of us possess dual citizenship in a physical country or colony and in an unseen one.

The fact is, those of us who are known as Kingdom colonists are not earthlings; we are "heavenlings."

Since Kingdom of God is a country, a real place called Heaven, and since countries bestow citizenship on the people who dwell there, it is citizenship (not membership) that has been bestowed on the "heavenlings" who dwell on the colony called Earth. Citizenship comes with more guarantees and privileges than membership does, along with specific responsibilities.

You can become a member of a *community* within your colony or country, but your citizenship is what ties you to the community in the first place. In the same way, you can become a member of a religion or a branch of a religion, but your citizenship in the kingdom of light (or, sad to say, the kingdom of darkness) will take priority over your membership in that particular religion.

Naturalized citizenship is the goal, not mere membership, whether you live in the primary country or one of its colonies. You need to pursue full citizenship in the Kingdom of Heaven as if your life depended upon it, because it does.

As a citizen, you will grow to reflect the culture of the country, which in turn reflects the ruler of the country. Your life will be radically changed and improved as a result. Citizenship is a legal position. Membership is more of an accommodation. You can apply for membership in the local

lodge or Rotary Club and they can decide whether or not to accommodate and include you. They can also decide to demember (I could have written dis-member) you, making you a non-member. But once you are a citizen, no one can take away your citizenship just because they don't like you, not even the government. (You can read how this applies to a citizen of the Kingdom of Heaven in John 10:28-29.)

Having legal citizenship entitles you to certain rights, and those rights do not depend on feelings or emotions; they depend on much more powerful things: position and law. You can switch religious affiliations or other memberships without losing your citizenship in the Kingdom, and people do. They get their feelings hurt or they offend somebody, so they move on. They change their minds about what they want to do, so they find a new place that will accommodate their viewpoint.

Declaration of Independence

Now even though a country will not remove your name from the citizenship rolls, a citizen can remove his own name if he or she chooses. In any kind of kingdom, that is called rebellion, and it happens all the time. When the American colonists wrote their Declaration of Independence, they were announcing their intention to renounce their

English citizenship, to break off legal ties with that country, to establish their own independent nation.

Once you are a citizen, no one can take away your citizenship just because they don't like you, not even the government.

Independence and private ownership are an abomination within a colony. They cannot coexist with a kingdom mentality. To this day, the "American spirit" is the same as a spirit of independence, and a strong streak of individualism and private ownership has resulted in the growth of capitalism and its inherent conflicts. Please do not misunderstand me; I am American, I love America, it is the land of the free and home of the brave, and a place where anyone, can become anything... but it has also become a place that rejects the concept of authority. This is due to the strongholds that have developed over the centuries. And I know some are having an issue with my even making this statement; but we must come to the understanding that all freedom without authority is anarchy, especially in the Kingdom.

When the first man declared independence from his government in the Garden, he resigned his citizenship by switching it to the kingdom of darkness (darkness is synonymous with ignorance).

Adam was ignorant of the importance of obedience to the single legal regulation of his government, and he was ignorant of the goals of his government.

Once saved always saved? A declaration of independence results in the loss of citizenship. You may not even know what you are doing, but the end result is the same. If you change your mind, you may decide to seek citizenship again, and you may eventually be repatriated. But it will not be easy to regain your citizenship once you have lost it. Just a note here about what the human race lost when the first human being declared his independence from his original King. We need to know what we are looking for if we ever hope to regain it. The human race did not lose residence in Heaven. The first human was created on earth and out of the earth. His residence was on earth. He never resided in Heaven and he did not fall from Heaven. He was the original colonist, and he had been allotted full citizenship in the Kingdom of Heaven even as he dwelt on the earth. What he rejected was his *assignment*, which was to exercise dominion over the earth in obedience to the King. When he refused to follow God's directions in fulfilling his assignment, that first man lost dominion and citizenship at the same time.

As the story goes, Adam's wife, Eve, was persuaded by a talking serpent, otherwise known as the devil, to eat some delicious-looking fruit from one of the trees in their garden paradise. Trouble was, that was the one and only thing their Creator-King, God, had instructed them *not* to do. They had only one rule and they broke it. So they got kicked out of their garden, and all of their children, grandchildren, and so forth were born outside of the colony territory—which means that

none of them were born into citizenship in the Kingdom of Heaven.

Because of what the first man did, every one of the 7.3 billion people on earth and the 259,000 who were born last night are hungry for the Kingdom of God. It is not about going to Heaven someday (although most religions think so); it is about becoming restored into the Kingdom that our long ago forefather lost. It is about resuming exercise of the dominion over the planet, expanding the original colony until it covers the entire globe.

Habakkuk 2:14

> *For the earth shall be filled with the knowledge of the glory of the LORD, as the waters cover the sea.*

In the Garden, the first man had it all. He had every provision and all the privileges that come with the assignment of stewardship and management. The Garden was the first settlement of the colony of Heaven, and the Fall changed all that. We call this "the Fall" and yet we do not really think very much about what those first humans fell from. Innocence? Goodness? Obedience? Yes, but more importantly they fell from <u>dominion</u>. They fell down on the job by breaking the one rule or law they had been given. For two bites of fruit, they lost their citizenship in the colony of the Kingdom of Heaven. Through the Fall, Earth was disconnected from Heaven. No longer did Adam defer to the direction of God.

It is about resuming exercise of the dominion over the planet, expanding the original colony until it covers the entire globe.

High Treason

The first man's decision to disregard God's prohibition and to eat of the fruit of the tree seems like such a minor thing. But God regarded it as high treason. Treason involves deceit and corruption. The highest form of trust has been broken. Adam not only disobeyed the one rule he had been given, he lied about it afterward.

If an ambassador of a country should sell the secrets of his country to another country, that is treason. In every country in the world, treason is punishable by death. That is why God, when He gave Adam the whole world to run, entrusted all of it to his stewardship, but gave him the one single prohibition, and leveled with him about the potential punishment: "You must not eat from the tree of the knowledge of good and evil, for when you eat from it you will certainly die" (Gen. 2:17, NIV). The pronouncement of the punishment of death revealed the gravity of the sin. *The word sin means rebellion against authority.* Now Adam and all of the individuals who followed

him would find death inevitable. He had committed treason. The man himself could not undo the punishment. A new Adam would have to come from Heaven to do that, and He did. He came to restore what Adam lost—everything.

What is Citizenship?

Many people who migrate to America from other countries know that legal citizenship status can be hard to get and that people must want it badly enough to work for it. They know that American

citizenship would provide them with opportunities they cannot have any other way.

By definition, a "citizen" is someone who owes allegiance to a government and who is therefore entitled to receive protection from mistreatment and also to enjoy special rights and privileges that come with citizenship. A citizen is automatically connected with the seat of power of his

government. That is why people want to become citizens of successful and wealthy nations; once you are a citizen you can expect your life to improve. Why else would you want to go to all that trouble?

Citizenship is the most valuable asset of a nation. Because of its power, it is not easily given or obtained and the current citizens of a nation do not readily want to share citizenship with outsiders. We are seeing this play out in many countries at the present time because of the continuing influx of immigrants from Muslim countries. Such a large population shift has the potential to transform the entire religious, social, and cultural complexion of the nation. The Muslim immigrants would not be moving into those countries if they did not offer the prospect of a higher standard of living.

Here in the United States, we also hear reports of Mexican immigration challenges. In spite of checkpoints and an actual fence on the U.S.-Mexican border, illegal immigrants pour into the southwestern states and move northward. Some legislators want to place all illegal aliens on a fast track to American citizenship. Others want to detain and deport them.

Citizenship is such a valuable status that people are willing to do wicked things to obtain it. They falsify documents or marry people they do not even know simply to get the advantages of citizenship. All immigrants, legal or otherwise, are seeking the privileges and benefits of the host country. They want jobs, higher pay, better health care, greater educational opportunities, and an overall better quality of life than they can obtain as citizens of their home countries. The best way to obtain improved benefits and rights is to become full citizens of a successful and well-to-do nation.

A citizen is part of an elite, privileged group, and people who were born into their citizenship do not appreciate their status as much as they could. Citizenship is easy to come by if you are born into it, but if you must seek naturalized citizenship you soon find out that it can be an arduous process. Citizenship status is too precious for governments to hand out indiscriminately like handbills.

You need to know that the benefits of citizenship in a country with a kingdom system of government can far outweigh the benefits of citizenship in even wealthy nations that have non-kingdom forms of government. This is because, ideally, the king's wealth will be distributed broadly to his citizens, whereas in a democratic country where capitalism prevails, not everyone can capitalize on the resources to the same degree. (In fact, poverty is necessary for capitalism to work, because you need "have-nots" to sell products and services to.)

Now, I personally had a hard time grasping this understanding because I am a hard working American citizen, an entrepreneur and business person as well as a minister, and I have always treasured capitalism (prior to my Kingdom understanding) because I knew that my hands and my mind and my power and my enthusiasm and my hard work and my dedication will allow me to succeed. Do you see a common thread in MY paragraph?

The Kingdom of God is a perfect Commonwealth where you do not have to work or toil for it's benefits, they are freely provided simply because you are a citizen. A citizen of a kingdom who is in good standing with a king has more than enough of everything.

But seek ye first the kingdom of God, and his righteousness; and all these things shall be added unto you.

Seek and find the Kingdom of God, become a citizen there, and all other kingdoms become subservient to you because your King is the King of Kings and Lord of Lords and you belong to Him as a part of His Kingdom. Will He not take care of his own?

Power of Citizenship

Citizenship empowers an individual; citizenship provides legitimate access to all the rights and privileges of a constitution and a country. Becoming a citizen, especially a citizen of a kingdom such as the Kingdom of God, means that you become powerful. Your citizenship is the source of your personal authority where those rights are concerned. You have the power to demand things. By the power of your citizenship, you can call in constitutional privileges and promises. The

constitution is more powerful than the citizens, just as the law is more powerful than the lawyer or the judge that exercises it and certainly more powerful than the politicians who talk about it. Good citizens have access to the full protection and advantage of the law.

A citizen of a kingdom who is in good standing with a king has more than enough of everything. The king sets the standards—and he makes it possible for his citizens to achieve them. Remember our definition of a kingdom: A kingdom is the governing influence of a king over a territory, impacting that territory with his will, his purpose, and his intent, producing a culture and a moral standard for his citizens. Notice...these benefits belong only to his citizens. Citizenship matters greatly. An individual's welfare depends on it.

Remember what we learned about citizenship vs. membership. Countries do not have members. You cannot be a member of the United States of America. You cannot be a member of Jamaica. You can certainly be a member of a religious group or an organization, but you would never say

that you are a member of a country because membership does not entitle you to the full range of rights. Citizens have rights, and they do not have to pay membership dues to keep them.

Citizenship is permanent, if you want it to be. Whether or not the people around you like you, you cannot be deprived of your constitutional rights by a consensus or somebody's whim. Once you are a citizen, you are no longer a mere member; you are a legal creature, which means the law protects you. You could even say that citizenship is dangerous. Law means you remove emotions and relationships out of the equation. It doesn't matter who you like or do not like, or who likes you. You are a citizen, regardless.

Citizens have rights, and they do not have to pay membership dues to keep them. Citizenship is

permanent, if you want it to be. Citizenship is the most powerful gift that a government can give an individual.

You can learn the language of a country and still not have citizenship. You can obtain a working visa and earn money in a country and remain an alien. You can live for decades in a place and never become a citizen. Only by going all the way through the citizenship initiation process can you become a citizen. For your part as a citizen, you need to submit to the rules and regulations of your government. For the government's part, it agrees to take you in and give you powerful entitlements. You can only become a citizen when the government opts to make an agreement with you.

Behind citizenship lies a covenant—a legal contract or solemn agreement—between the government and each individual citizen. Citizens, in other words, have a contract with their government.

That citizenship covenant gives you so much power that you can even attack the government. Governments know this, which is one of the reasons they do not give citizenship to everybody who walks by the immigration office. Citizenship is the most powerful gift, to use the term broadly, that a government can give an individual. The constitution of the government (Your bible) guarantees certain valuable rights to its citizens, and each and every citizen has access to the same rights. Citizens must maintain their access to those rights by complying with a common set of laws. When you move to another country, you do not bring your own laws with you. You must submit to that country's laws day in and day out if you expect to carry out your part of the bargain. All covenants or contracts have two parties, and the contract of citizenship is no exception. The citizen's part of the agreement is to comply with the law of the land.

Those rights are guaranteed to you. You do not have to beg for them. You do not have to bribe anybody to manipulate favor. Once you become a citizen of a country, you are responsible to the government to follow the laws. The government is responsible for protecting your rights, but you

always remain accountable for your behavior. If you transgress, you may find yourself deprived of some of your rights for a while. When people go to prison, their citizenship does not get revoked, but some of the rights and privileges do —because they did not hold up their side of the contract as law-abiding citizens.

In a very real way, citizenship is power-sharing. A citizen shares the power of the government. Essentially, a citizen becomes one with the government. (A negative example of this power would be when an elected government suddenly extends citizenship to a group of people who will then vote them back into power.) No greater honor can be bestowed on an individual than the honor or making him or her citizen.

Luke 10:20

> *Notwithstanding in this rejoice not, that the spirits are subject unto you; but rather rejoice, because your names are written in heaven.*

A government could give you a piece of property, and it would not be as secure as citizenship because they could take it back and expel you. They could give you a visa to live in the country for six months, but at the end of that time, you would have to leave. They could give you a five-year working permit and yet you would not be able to exercise the rights of citizenship—and at any time during that five years, they could change their minds, write a new law, and tell you to go home immediately. Citizenship is a privilege, after all. You can't just have it for the asking.

Citizenship is the conferring of a nation on an individual. They take the whole country and they put it on top of you. You walk in with nothing and you leave with everything on you.

Here is my best definition of citizenship:

Citizenship is the constitutional rights and privileges bestowed upon an individual, guaranteeing legal status to the individual, which is protected by the laws of the country.

Submit to the constitutional laws and codes of conduct of your nation. Not only will you stay out of trouble, you will reinforce your claim on the rights and benefits that are yours by virtue of your citizenship status. As part of entering more completely into your precious citizenship, you may decide to take a look at a copy of the constitution of your country, in spite of the fact that its legal

terminology may be difficult to comprehend. Most people never do this. Many people do not even think about the fact that their citizenship is controlled by a document called a constitution.

If you are a citizen living in a colony, you do not have to wait until you can travel to the country that colonized your region. You can experience your citizenship right where you are.

Now it's true that people can interpret the same constitution in different ways, but that does not make it powerless. It is also true that the constitution of your country was written by legislators who are more than likely very elderly if not already dead, so nobody can consult them and get the

final word about what they intended when they chose the wording. Nevertheless, it is the only constitution you have, unless you claim dual citizenship.

Keep the word "constitution" in mind as you continue to read this book, because I want to make another important point about it later. This is a book about the most special kind of citizenship you can possess, and the attributes of your national citizenship can help you understand your Kingdom citizenship.

VII

Kingdom Mandates & Laws

- 21 Spiritual Laws of the Kingdom-

The difference between a lake and a swamp is borders. The lake has defined borders that tell the water when and where to stop, the swamp does not. Defined borders are vital to society; and while physical borders are essential for any territory, I am addressing here the borders of moral, spiritual and personal aspects. We all want freedom, but freedom without authority is anarchy. This is what has led to the moral decay of society today and the increasing lawlessness that is and will abound as the time of the end draws closer (Mat 24:12).

For years the bible (our Kingdom Constitution) has been the moral compass and guide for morality in America. But sadly the populous no longer wants this, nor do they deem it even appropriate or respectful to their other many false religions that have been let in to flourish. So what does that mean? Then who defines right from wrong? What constant is there to define the line between moral and immoral? The Word of God teaches us not to kill, steal, how to treat our neighbors.. Let's go further, and not to have sexual intercourse with our same sex or animals... Take the Constitution away and where's the line? Maybe the next generation will say it's ok to have intercourse with 3 year olds, or to just do as you please with and to anyone as long as it makes you feel good. I know it sounds extreme, but it is not. I'll say it again, freedom without authority is anarchy.

Just as every Kingdom has a King, and borders, every Kingdom has laws; it is through your citizenship of the Kingdom, which is obtained solely by righteousness and cannot be earned, that gives you rights to declare the benefits of the Kingdom. We must understand that while all benefits are made available to all citizens, not all are without action on your part. There are things such as protection from the enemy, which even includes a Kingdom language that the enemy cannot decode, unconditional love, forgiveness and acceptance are all free and available to everyone who wishes to be a part of the Kingdom of God.

The Kingdom has tools, special gifts and even appointments (ministry, fivefold, etc..) that are available to every citizen, but they must step into these, or just like governmental benefits in the world, if you do not take them, they will sit and someone else may step in (more on this later).

Just as there are natural and physical laws that rule and control our outcomes, there are also spiritual laws that control our eternal destiny within the Kingdom. Any organization in order to be successful requires structure and laws and so it is in God's spiritual Kingdom. God operates under a set of strict spiritual laws that I would say most Christians do not understand.

In order to understand spiritual laws, you must first start by recognizing that there are spiritual laws. But wait, you say you have been redeemed from the law… yes, the laws of Moses, from the commandments of the Law, you are free; but it's important to know that this is not that. There are spiritual principles and laws that even God stands by and these are perpetual laws of the Kingdom.

Each one of these laws work in your favor when you acknowledge them, or against you when you don't. Conversely, you may be operating according to a spiritual law and either not know it, or in the inverse of its intended purpose, but in either case, you will reap what the law (principle) purposed.

Its funny to me that in researching this, I came across articles that say there are 21 "universal laws" of the world... And I have counted 21 laws that God lays out in His Word, each with a guaranteed result if followed. I want to start off with what I believe to be the chief 4 and spend some time with them, them flow through the remainder.

Spiritual Law 1: The Law of Redemption

> Galatians 3:13*Christ hath redeemed us from the curse of the law, being made a curse for us: for it is written, Cursed is every one that hangeth on a tree:*

Spiritual Law 2: The Law of Faith

> *Rom 3:27 Where is boasting then? It is excluded. By what law? of works? Nay: but by the law of faith.*

Spiritual Law 3: Sin and Death vs. Spirit and Life

> *Rom 8:2 For the law of the Spirit of life in Christ Jesus hath made me free from the law of sin and death.*

Spiritual Law 4: Sowing & Reaping

> *Gen 8:22 While the earth remaineth, seedtime and harvest, and cold and heat, and summer and winter, and day and night shall not cease.*

> *Gal 6:7 Be not deceived; God is not mocked: for whatsoever a man soweth, that shall he also reap.*

OK, before listing all of them, I want to take more time discussing the first four, because they are paramount to Kingdom understanding. It is important to know that one does not cancel out the other, they work together. Getting a revelation in one area and negating another will leave you barren in that area.

Hosea 4:6

My people are destroyed for lack of knowledge:

Ignorance will cost you. Not having knowledge in an area will cost you dearly so as the wisest man to ever live put it in Proverbs 18:1: *The heart of the prudent getteth knowledge; and the ear of the wise seeketh knowledge.* I am giving you knowledge here and ask that with all your knowledge, get understanding. So I am reminding you that as you continue to read, put away your limiting beliefs and knowledge and open your mind to understanding. Because when we have knowledge in limited areas we form religious strongholds that hold us back from a fullness of understanding in other areas because we believe that what we presently know, is the fullness of the gospel, and there is always more. I am reiterating this here because the areas below are areas of contention for religious spirits and groups and I want to put that spirit in check before moving forward. So if this is you today, please put the book down, pray for God to reveal only His truth to you and pray in spirit for 2 minutes than come back and continue.

Spiritual Law 1: The Law of Redemption

As a believer, one of the most powerful revelations you can have is to fully understand that you have been "redeemed from the curse of the law" because it is a huge key to a life of victory!

Galatians 3:13 says, "*Christ has redeemed us FROM THE CURSE OF THE LAW.* If we are to experience victory every day of our life we need to understand this truth and what it means to us.

Redeem means to purchase back or to buy up. It means to rescue from loss or to ransom. When you pay a ransom for something you pay a price in order to get someone or something back.

It is the grace of God that Jesus paid the price to release us from the curse of the law, to free us from the devil's authority (Colossians 1:13), and to bring us back into His kingdom – with all its privileges and benefits including victory in our life. We are purchased by His precious blood and as a result, we are brought back to Father God.

What Are We Redeemed From?

We are redeemed from the "curse of the law", but what exactly is the curse of the law? There are three major areas the curse of the law impacts the human race:

Curse of Spiritual Death.

Spiritual death is separation from God. Without Jesus, you are lost, separated from the Father, and spiritually dead. The moment you accept Jesus as your Lord and Savior you receive ETERNAL LIFE with God. You become alive spiritually, a child of God, and as a result forever a citizen of the Kingdom of God. Your sins are forgiven and you become a "NEW CREATION" in Christ. (2Corinthians 5:17) You are redeemed from the curse of spiritual death.

Curse of Sickness & Disease.

Sickness and disease are a curse. They are part of the curse of the fall and part of the curse of the law. The earth remains under a curse because of the fall of man in the garden of Eden, but through Christ, you are redeemed from the curse of the "Law". *"By His stripes, you WERE healed"*. (1Peter 2:24) Jesus has provided healing for every sickness and disease just like He provided forgiveness for every sin. Psalms 103:2-3 says, *"forget not all his benefits—who forgives all your sins and heals all your diseases,"*. You are redeemed from the curse of sickness and disease.

Curse of Poverty.

Poverty is a curse, not a blessing. The Word of God emphatically teaches that poverty is a curse (Deut. 28:16-19,38-40). And the Word of God teaches that Christ redeemed us from that curse. He redeemed us from poverty so we wouldn't have to live in poverty and lack in this life.

2 Corinthians 8:9 says, *"For ye know the grace of our Lord Jesus Christ, that, though he was rich, yet for your sake, he became poor, that ye through his poverty might be made rich."*

Your redemption is far-reaching. When you realize Christ has redeemed you from spiritual death, poverty, and sickness you'll be able to experience everything that belongs to you – peace, joy, freedom from guilt, shame, and condemnation. You will be walk in victory every day or your life.

Notice our redemption is in the past tense – *Christ has redeemed us* – we have already been redeemed! We don't need to be hoping and praying for, or trying to convince God to do something. He has already done it – "IT IS FINISHED". The work of redemption from the curse of the law has already been established through Christ being cursed for us.

Walk-in Victory & Enjoy the Blessings

Christ paid the price in full for your redemption. Now it is up to you to believe and receive. Notice it doesn't say the curse is no longer there. The curse is still all around us. You can see it throughout the world. But now you have a choice. You can in the Name of Jesus the King, walk-in victory by grace through faith.

Don't allow the devil to deceive you and intimidate you with fear, guilt, and condemnation. God wants you to enjoy the blessing He has provided. Choose to live the abundant, prosperous, overcoming, and victorious life. How? By knowing you've been redeemed from the curse of the Law by the blood of Jesus Christ. Stand on God's Word and claim the blessing of Abraham that is yours in Christ. You are a citizen of the Kingdom of God, so know your rights.

God's already done it. He sent Jesus to redeem you from the curse. The rest is up to you. I hear people saying, and even pastors preaching that it's all done by grace, and I need to do nothing but accept it. That is very true, but if you accept it and do nothing with it, you are as an unprofitable steward and servant. Now you must appropriate what has already been done for you. Believe it, walk in it and receive it. It is a key to living the life of victory every day of your life!

Also, before moving forward please understand also that the laws listed below are principles. Just because they are labeled laws does not redeem you from them! They are principles put into motion by the King for the operation of His Kingdom. Whatever area you do not operate in the specific principle/law, does not disqualify you from the others or their benefits. It is just like your government, if they have benefits to citizens and you do not know about them or take advantage of them, you will not reap the reward of it, but it will not disqualify you from accessing any other areas as a citizen.

Spiritual Law 2: The Law of Faith

The initial citizenship card that you receive to enter and become a citizen of the Kingdom of God is because you made a decision to receive

Jesus Christ as your Lord and personal Savior. You did this by faith. Just as Adam sinned and all mankind was born into sin as a result, Paul explains that it is by one Mans (Jesus Christ) obedience that you were made righteous. In other words, the only thing you need to do to be permitted into the Kingdom is become born again. John 3:3 Jesus states: "...unless one is born again, he cannot see the kingdom of God.". This decision to be born again is the first most important Kingdom decision you will ever make, and it is all done by faith.

We know that it is impossible to please God without faith, and we want to be pleasing to our King, so I will spend a little more time on this law than the others...

The apostle Paul said,

Romans 3:27

> *Where is boasting then? It is excluded. By what law? Of works? Nay: **but by the law of faith***

When we look at natural or scientific laws, like the law of gravity, or the law of aerodynamics, or Newton's laws of motion, they are laws that work consistently every time without fail (assuming nothing supernatural intervenes). Faith also is a law which when operated properly works every time without fail. By using the law of faith we can obtain any of the promises of God, including healing, deliverance from sin, forgiveness of sins, justification, and salvation. It works on the same basis as natural laws such as the law of gravity work, and that is that God ordains that it works, "upholding all things by the word of His power" (Heb 1:3)

Faith is the means by which we can obtain any of the promises of God, and there are some basic conditions for faith in God to work. These do not all apply in every case, but most of them will.

1. We must base our faith on what God has said, or on what we know he will do.
2. Sometimes we must ask God for it.
3. Sometimes we must command it to happen.
4. We must believe that we receive what we ask for or command to happen.
5. We must confess what we believe.
6. We must act upon what we believe and confess, by fulfilling any conditions which apply to the situation concerned.
7. We must endure through any time period that God ordains before the manifestation of the promise.

In this section, I will explain the scriptural basis for the law of faith to work for any Christian; or better put, the Constitutional foundation of the Law of Faith. The law must be in the Constitution, so faith must be based upon what God has said:

Numbers 23:19

> *19 God is not a man, that he should lie; neither the son of man, that he should repent: has he said, and shall he not do it? Or has he spoken and shall he not make it good?*

Isaiah 14:24

> *24 Yahweh of Hosts has sworn, saying, Surely as I have thought, so shall it come to pass; and as I have purposed, so shall it stand:*

Isaiah 46:11

> *Calling a ravenous bird from the east, the man who executes my council from a far country; yes, I have spoken it, I will also bring it to pass; I have purposed it, I will also do it.*

Jeremiah 4:28

For this shall the earth mourn, and the heavens above be black; <u>because I have spoken it, I have purposed it, and will not repent, neither will I turn back from it.</u>

Ezekiel 12:25

<u>*For I am Yahweh: I will speak, and the word that I shall speak shall come to pass; it shall be no more prolonged:*</u> *for in your days, O rebellious house, <u>will I say the word, and will perform it, says the Lord Yahweh.</u>*

Ezekiel 22:14

Can your heart endure, or can your hands be strong in the days that I shall deal with you? <u>I Yahweh have spoken it, and will do it.</u>

Ezekiel 36:36

Then the heathen that are left round about you shall know that I Yahweh build the ruined places, and plant that which was desolate: <u>I Yahweh have spoken it, and I will do it.</u>

1 John 5:14-15

[14] And this is the confidence that we have in him, that, <u>if we ask anything according to his will, he hears us;</u>

[15] <u>And if we know that he hears us, whatever we ask, we know that we have the petitions we desired of him.</u>"

Note: Everyone has faith in something. If we go to catch a bus, we believe that it will come. We prepare our fare, go to the bus stop before the expected time of arrival, and wait for it. We may look expectantly along the road in the direction we expect the bus to come from, and when it comes it is not a surprise. We have faith that the driver knows how to drive, and he will not crash the bus. We have faith that the bus has been serviced properly, and it will not crash because of mechanical failure of some sort. This kind of faith is based upon what we know about the bus company; whether they keep to their timelines or not, whether they regularly check the fitness and capability of the drivers, and employ well-trained mechanics to service the buses. This is natural faith, but when it comes to faith in God, we are not putting our trust in things we can see, but in an invisible God, and what we believe he has said.

This is possible even in the natural realm. Imagine a man who opens a trap door in the floor of his house and goes down into the cellar. There is no light down there apart from the light that comes through the trap door, and his small daughter comes and shouts to him, "Daddy, are you down there?"

He replies, "Yes, dear."

She asks, "Can I come down there to you?"

He replies, "Yes, dear, just sit on the edge of the trap door and jump, and I will catch you."

The little girl sits on the edge of the trap door and looks down. She sees nothing but darkness. She says, "Daddy, I cannot see you."

He replies, "No, dear, but I can see you, just jump and I will catch you."

Believing the words of her father, whom she cannot see, she jumps into the darkness, and lands safely in his arms.

She had faith in her father's words even though she could not see him, and this is how we need to be with God. The reason why we can base our faith on what God has said is because, as the above scriptures show, he has promised to bring to pass what he has said. Therefore, if the King has promised to do a certain thing for us, then providing we fulfill the conditions that he has laid down, he will bring it to pass:

(Numbers 23:19) "God is not a man that he should lie."

(Titus 1:2) "God ... cannot lie."

If we base our faith on something other than God's word, such as man's word, or circumstances, or things we can see, then we could have a faulty base, because these things can change. However, God has said, "My covenant will I not break, nor alter the thing that is gone out of my lips" (Psalm 89:34), and when we trust in what he has said, we have a sound base because, "he is faithful who promised" (Hebrews 10:23).

Ask and it Shall be Given unto You:

Matthew 7:7-8

> *7 <u>Ask, and it shall be given you;</u> seek, and you shall find; knock, and it shall be opened to you:*
>
> *8 <u>For every one who asks receives;</u> and he who seeks finds; and to him who knocks it shall be opened.*

James 1:6-7

> *6 But let him ask in faith, nothing wavering. For he who wavers is like a wave of the sea driven with the wind and tossed.*

7 For do not let that man think that he shall receive any thing of the Lord.

Note: We do not have to ask for everything. Many people become believers in Jesus without asking for it. Some even get baptized in the Holy Spirit without asking for it - Cornelius and his household were examples of this (Acts 10:44-46). Abraham never asked for his seed to become as numerous as the stars of heaven (Genesis 15:5), but God still promised it to him. Nevertheless, many times we do need to ask, *because not asking is often the reason why we do not receive anything from God:*

James 4:2

> *...ye have not, because ye ask not.*

Another reason why sometimes we do not receive from God is because there is unrepentant sin in our lives:

Psalm 66:18

> *If I regard iniquity in my heart, Yahweh will not hear me:*

Notice who regards the iniquity? It's not God. We hold ourselves in contempt and back from receiving many times; and this is the result:

Isaiah 59:2

> *But your iniquities have separated between you and your God, and your sins have hid his face from you, that he will not hear.*

What is important to remember, is not to let a particular sin weigh you down and keep you from obtaining the promises. Everyone falls short, but thank God for His forgiveness, grace and love which restores us to righteousness. Unrepentant sin however, is treated differently in the Kingdom. The Kingdom has laws and we must abide by those laws to achieve the benefits of that particular law. Citizen hear me, because I am not referring to the Law of sin and death, or spirit and life, we will get into that in a bit and how they intertwine with this, but if you are being convicted of something in your spirit, it will hold you back from certain areas of access in the Kingdom because just like earthy politics (or at least the way it should be), the more authority you yield, the more spotless you should be and the more accountable to the King you are (Luke 12:48). And I know that this is not easy for many religious people who believe everything revolves around grace (and in a sense it does), but without betting yourself bound up by law, understand that *"For unto whomsoever much is given, of him shall be much required"*.

You will not live your life like hell, or in a way that is not reflective of the Kingdom and expect the endowment of the Kingdom to be upon your life. This is what Jesus meant in John 3:3 when Jesus said *"except a man be born again, he cannot see the kingdom of God"*. We religiously take this to mean and preach it with salvation, but that is not what Jesus is speaking of in the scripture. Nicodemus made a statement to Jesus concerning His ability to perform miracles, Jesus answered and said unto him, *"Verily, verily, I say unto thee, Except a man be born again, he cannot see the Kingdom of God"*. So then what is He saying? Unless you are a physical man/woman who has taken on the government (through the acceptance and allegiance to the Governor, our Holy Spirit) of the Kingdom, you cannot access the Kingdom.

OK, I sidetracked, good thing I wasn't preaching! By the books end, we will come full circle with all of this, so let's move forward!!

Sometimes we must Command

Matthew 17:19-21

> *19 Then the disciples came to Jesus apart, and said, Why could not we cast him out?*
>
> *20 And Jesus said to them, <u>Because of your unbelief</u>; for amen I say to you, <u>If you have faith as a grain of mustard seed, you shall say to this mountain, Remove from here to there; and it shall remove; and nothing shall be impossible to you.</u>*
>
> *21 However this kind does not go out but by prayer and fasting.*

Mark 11:23

> *23 For amen I say to you, That whoever shall say to this mountain, Be removed, and be cast into the sea; and shall not doubt in his*

heart, but shall believe that those things which he says shall come to pass; whatever he says shall be his.

Here we see a different use of faith. There are times, such as when we cast demons out of people, that we should command, rather than ask, using the authority that Jesus gave us:

Matthew 10:1

And when He had called his twelve disciples to him, He gave them authority over unclean spirits to cast them out, and to heal every sickness and every disease.

Luke 9:1

Then He called his twelve disciples together, and gave them power and authority over all demons, and to cure diseases.

Luke 10:19

Behold, I give you the authority to tread on serpents and scorpions, and over all the power of the enemy.

However, it seems obvious that prayer should precede the commanding for it to work, because Jesus sometimes prayed all night (Luke 6:12) before he went out to do these works. When the disciples could not cast a certain demon out (Mat 17:19), Jesus told them that it was because of their unbelief (Mat 17:20), and they needed to pray and fast (Mat 17:21). Peter knelt down and prayed before he commanded the dead Tabitha (Dorcas) to arise (Acts 9:40). There are other reasons to consider why sometimes it will not work:

1. Disobedience to God's word. If we do not honor and obey God's word, then we show that it does not have authority in our

lives, and if we do not obey it, why should we expect the devil to obey it?

2. Sin in our lives. If we live in sin then we allow the devil to have authority over us, and therefore he does not necessarily have to obey our words:

Proverbs 22:12

Yahweh ... he overthrows the words of the transgressor."

Hosea 14:9

The ways of Yahweh are right, and the just shall walk in them, but the transgressors shall fall in them.

3. Failure to honor our own words. If we say that we are going to do certain things, and then do not do them, and we show no respect or obedience to our own words, then why should we expect the devil to obey them?

My brothers and sisters, this has nothing to do with salvation and everything to do with your authority. If you want to operate at a higher level, you must live at a higher level.

Let's turn up the faith.. We must believe that we are receiving when we pray or Command

Mathew 21:22

> *And all things, whatever you shall ask in prayer, believing, you shall receive.*

Mark 11:23-24

> *²³ For amen I say to you, That whoever shall say to this mountain, Be removed, and be cast into the sea; and shall not doubt in his heart, but shall believe that those things which he says come to pass1; he shall have whatever he says.*

24 Therefore I say to you, Whatever things you ask, when you pray, believe that you receive them, and they shall be yours.

There are two things that these scriptures tell us that we need to believe. First, that what we say comes to pass. If we pray and believe that God has answered our prayer, then we need to believe that the manifestation of what we say either happens, or is happening, or is a certainty, because if we believe it, God has said that he will bring our words to pass. Second, that we receive what we ask for when we pray. You may ask, "How can I believe that I receive when I don't have it?"

1 John 5:14-15

> *And this is the confidence that we have in him, that, if we ask anything according to his will, he hears us;*
>
> *And if we know that he hear, whatever we ask, we know that we have the petitions we asked of him."*

Once you have faith and believe, you must confess what you believe:

Matthew 10:32-33

> *32 Whoever therefore shall confess1 me before men, him will I confess also before my Father who is in heaven.*
>
> *33 But whoever shall deny me before men, him will I also deny before my Father who is in heaven.*

Matthew 17:19-21

> *19 Then the disciples came to Jesus apart, and said, Why could not we cast him out?*
>
> *20 And Jesus said to them, Because of your unbelief; for amen I say to you, If you have faith as a grain of mustard seed, you shall say*

to this mountain, Remove from here to yonder place; and it shall remove; and nothing shall be impossible to you.

²¹ However this kind does not go out but by prayer and fasting.

Matthew 21:21

> *²¹ Jesus answered and said to them, Amen I say to you, If You have faith and doubt not, you shall not only do this which is done to the fig tree, but also if you shall say to this mountain, Be removed, and be cast into the sea; it shall be done.*

Mark 11:22-23

> *²² And Jesus answering says unto them, Have faith in God.*
>
> *²³ For amen I say to you, That whoever shall say to this mountain, Be removed, and be cast into the sea; and shall not doubt in his heart, but shall believe that those things which he says shall come to pass; he shall have whatever he says.*

Romans 10:9-10

> *⁹ That if you shall confess with your mouth the Lord Jesus, and shall believe in your heart that God has raised him from the dead, you shall be saved.*
>
> *¹⁰ For with the heart man believes to righteousness, and with the mouth confession is made to salvation.*

2 Corinthians 4:13

> *¹³ We having the same Spirit of faith, according as it is written, I believed, and therefore I have spoken; we also believe, and therefore speak.*

Paul said that he spoke what he believed (2 Cor 4:13), but why is it so necessary to do this? The mountains don't move by believing they will move, and just looking at them, do they? They also have to be spoken to (Mat 17:20; 21:21; Mark 11:23).Demons don't come out just by believing that they will, and just looking at the person oppressed: <u>words have to be spoken</u> (Luke 4.36; Luke 8.29; Luke 13:12; Acts 16:18). The reason is that words are spirit, just as Jesus said, *"the words that I speak to you, they are Spirit and they are life"* (John 6:63), and if we want the Spirit of God to move in our situation, then we must speak the Word of God out of our mouths just as Jesus did. When we do this with a believing heart, God will bring to pass what we speak:

Proverbs 12:6 *"the mouth of the upright shall deliver them."*

Proverbs 12:18 *"the tongue of the wise is health."*

Isaiah 57:19 *"I create the fruit of the lips."*

Mark 11:23 *"he shall have whatever he says."*

This inevitably involves us in "calling those things which are not as though they are" (Romans 4:17), because we will be believing and confessing those "things which cannot be seen" (2 Corinthians 4:18). As far as our salvation is concerned, we must confess and also confess Jesus (Matthew 10:32-33; Romans 10:9-10). The word translated confess1 in these scriptures (Gr. ὁμολογέω, Gtr. homologeo) comes from two words, ὁμος (Gtr. homos) which means "same", and λέγω, (Gtr. lego), "I speak", and so means "to speak the same thing", or "to agree with".

To confess Jesus before men therefore means to speak the same as your King Jesus before men, and this means speak aloud the terms of the Constitution and invoke the Name of the King (to speak the Word of God as Jesus did).

And then act on what we believe and confess, because if you say something, then do it, if you confess something and believe it, then walk in it.. if you pray for rain, you better not leave your umbrella home!

James 2:17-26

17 Even so faith, if it does not have works, is dead, being alone.

18 Yes, a man may say, You have faith, and I have works: show me your faith without your works, and I will show you my faith by my works.

19 You believe that there is one God; you do well: the demons also believe, and tremble.

20 But will you know, O vain man, that faith without works is dead?

21 Was not Abraham our father justified by works, when he had offered Isaac his son upon the altar?

22 Do you see how faith worked with his works, and by works was faith made perfect?

23 And the scripture was fulfilled which says, Abraham believed God, and it was imputed to him for righteousness: and he was called the friend of God.

24 You see then how that by works a man is justified, and not by faith only.

25 Likewise also was not Rahab the harlot justified by works, when she had received the messengers, and sent them out another way?

26 For as the body without the spirit is dead, so faith without works is dead also.

Acting upon what we believe and confess is a very important part of faith, and without it our faith is dead (James 2:17; 2:20; 2:26), and will obtain us nothing (James 1:6-7). Look at these examples:

1. Abraham was justified because he acted on his faith when he offered Isaac his son to God, believing that God would raise him from the dead (Hebrews 11:17-19; 2.21).
2. Rahab the harlot was justified because she acted on her faith, when she hid the spies and made a covenant with them (Joshua 2:1-14; James 2:25), believing that God had given the land to Israel (v9). If she had not done this she would have died with the rest of them in Jericho.
3. Naaman the Syrian was healed of his leprosy when he acted on his faith, by obeying Elisha's instruction (Kings 5:10), and dipped in the Jordan seven times (Kings 5:14). If he had not done this, he would not have been healed.
4. The ten lepers were healed as they acted on their faith (Luke 17:19), and went to show themselves to the priests in obedience to Jesus (Luke 17:14). If they had not done this, they would not have been healed.
5. The woman with the issue of blood was healed when she pressed through the crowd and touched the hem of Jesus' garment, believing that if she did this she would be made well (Matt 9:20-22; Mark 5:25-29). If she had not done it, she would not have been healed.
6. Noah and his family were saved from the flood because Noah acted on his faith and built the ark (Heb 11:7). If he had not done this, he would have drowned with the rest of them.
7. The walls of Jericho fell by faith, when Israel acted on their faith, and went round the city for seven days (Heb 11:30), in obedience to God's instructions (Joshua 6:3-5). If they had not done this, they would not have taken Jericho.

These examples all show that if we do not act according to what we say we believe, then our faith is dead, and we will get nothing from God. As far as our salvation is concerned, we must not only confess what we believe, but we must also act in accordance with what be believe and confess. This means that we must obey the words of Jesus, because we cannot fulfill his commands to love (Matt 22:36-40; John 3:11) without doing it (John 14:21-24; 5:2-3; 1:6). Jesus' words will judge us on the last day (John 12:48), and salvation is only for those who obey him (Heb 5:9).

Now, before we move on to the next law, let me advise the danger of not having faith. Yes, I said danger. Because the fact is, that not having faith is fear.

Hebrews 11:6

> But <u>without faith it is impossible to please him</u>: for he that cometh to God must believe that he is, and that he is a rewarder of them that diligently seek him.

Fear is the reciprocal of faith. In other words, what ever you fear, is tantamount to you having faith in its opposite ability to what you should be believing. Example: If I am afraid of a snake biting me, or afraid of getting and dying of COVID, or afraid I will not make my mortgage payment this month, then I am having faith in the snakes ability to harm me, in the ability of COVID affecting me and of death, and having faith that I will be in lack.

You have to know, that you know that you know that your God, your King, is according to Ephesians 3:20, able to do far exceedingly above all you can ask, think or imagine, then take that and put it to work for you because you are a citizen of the Kingdom of God and you have a right to tread upon serpents, to walk in divine health and for your King to supply all of your needs according to His riches in the Kingdom!

Spiritual Law 3: Sin and Death vs. Spirit and Life

The apostle Paul refers to the law of sin and death in

Romans 8:1–2

> *There is therefore now no condemnation to them which are in Christ Jesus, who walk not after the flesh, but after the Spirit.*
>
> *² For the law of the Spirit of life in Christ Jesus hath made me free from the law of sin and death.*

What is the "law of sin and death"?

In these verses, Paul contrasts two laws: the law of the Spirit and the law of sin and death. The law of the Spirit is the gospel or good news of Jesus, the message of new life through faith in the resurrected Christ. The law of sin and death is the Old Testament Law of God. The Law is holy, just and good (Romans 7:12), but, because we cannot keep God's Law on our own, the result is only sin and death for those under the Law.

Romans 7:5 explains Paul's focus on the Law as leading to sin and death: "For when we were in the realm of the flesh, the sinful passions aroused by the law were at work in us, so that we bore fruit for death." In contrast, the "way" or law of the Spirit is noted in Romans 7:6: "But now, by dying to what once bound us, we have been released from the law so that we serve in the new way of the Spirit, and not in the old way of the written code." The Law itself is not sinful (Romans 7:7). However, the Law defined sin and stirred up our natural rebellion against God's rules, resulting in sin and death.

Romans 7:10–11 speaks of how sin, death, and the Law are connected: "*I found that the very commandment that was intended to bring life actually brought death. For sin, seizing the opportunity afforded by the commandment, deceived me, and through the commandment put me to death."* This death refers to spiritual separation from God. Shackled by our depraved nature, we naturally opposed the Law, and we found that God's life-giving Word served only to sentence us to death. It is because of this, that Paul can refer to the Law as the "law of sin and death."

The conclusion of Romans 7 shows the need of the gospel to deliver us from the consequences of sin under the Law:

Romans 7:22–25

> *22 For I delight in the law of God after the inward man:*
>
> *23 But I see another law in my members, warring against the law of my mind, and bringing me into captivity to the law of sin which is in my members.*
>
> *24 O wretched man that I am! who shall deliver me from the body of this death?*
>
> *25 I thank God through Jesus Christ our Lord. So then with the mind I myself serve the law of God; but with the flesh the law of sin.*

The next chapter, Romans 8, begins by declaring there is no longer any condemnation or judgment for those who are in Christ. We have been released from the law of sin and death. Paul's argument from Romans 7 transitions in Romans 8 to a rejoicing over the change the gospel makes in the lives of those who believe in Jesus.

The chapter concludes by confirming, in the strongest terms possible, that believers can never be separated from God's love:

Romans 8:38–39 (ESV)

> *For I am convinced that neither death nor life, neither angels nor demons, neither the present nor the future, nor any powers, neither height nor depth, nor anything else in all creation, will be able to separate us from the love of God that is in Christ Jesus our Lord*

What is the Kingdom connection? No matter who you were before, what you have done or didn't do, there is nothing that can separate you from the sincere love of your King and He invites you to put away all of your past, to just lay it down at His feet and He will disregard it as if it never happened and give you Kingdom citizenship and opportunity to lay hold of all the benefits that the Kingdom has to offer. Say Praise God!

Spiritual Law 4: Sowing & Reaping

Gen 8:22

> *While the earth remaineth, seedtime and harvest, and cold and heat, and summer and winter, and day and night shall not cease.*

Gal 6:7

> *Be not deceived; God is not mocked: for whatsoever a man soweth, that shall he also reap.*

In my last book on Kingdom finances and economics, I took you to a place that stretched your thinking and comfort with the understanding that money is a counterfeit anointing and will try to steal everything the anointing of God provides in His Kingdom. By seeking the Kingdom first and putting your economy second, third or even last, you place yourself in a position for God, the King to take care of you financially. Here I want to go a little further and deeper because this is not a book on economics but one of the fullness and the actual heart of the

Kingdom. So with the understanding that our citizenship is in contrast to what we are taught in the kingdom of this world, let's go deeper!

What if I told you that God does **NOT** want you to reap what you've sown?

I used to think that whatever you sow, that explicitly will you reap, chiefly because Galatians 6:7 says *whatsoever a man soweth, that shall he also reap.* But upon further study I found that the whatsoever is meaning the same in kind.. not specific to the product being sown.. such as:

Psalm 126:5

They that sow in tears shall reap in joy.

Proverbs 22:8

He that soweth iniquity shall reap vanity:

Jeremiah 12:13

> *They have sown wheat, but shall reap thorns:* (Speaking of the wickedness in Jerusalem)

Amos 9:13

> *Behold, the days come, saith the Lord, that the plowman shall overtake the reaper, and the treader of grapes him that soweth seed; and the mountains shall drop sweet wine, and all the hills shall melt.*

Job 4:8

> *Even as I have seen, <u>they that plow iniquity, and sow wickedness, reap the same.</u>*

Galatians 6:8

> *For he that soweth to his flesh shall of the flesh reap corruption; but he that soweth to the Spirit shall of the Spirit reap life everlasting.*

Do you see it? This is what happens when you see scriptures in their full contextual relationship with the entire bible and not just cherry picking scripture as many have wrongly done for years. So knowing that, I think it even males 2 Corinthians 9:6 even more exciting because The harvest God provides is so much better than what I can even strategize for; especially when we realize the common root of the harvest!

2 Corinthians 9:6

> *But this I say, He which soweth sparingly shall reap also sparingly; and he which soweth bountifully shall reap also bountifully.*

Sowing and reaping is an eternal spiritual Kingdom principle that is described in the constitution. It is such a universal reality that many cultures and religions recognize it in some form (ever heard of "karma"?). The idea that "doing bad things results in bad happening to you" while "doing good things results in good happening to you" has been observed and taught for centuries. And since it's found throughout the Bible — especially within the Law — Christians have become very comfortable with it.

Nowhere do we talk about the topic of sowing and reaping more than when we're discussing money. We're often told that when we give, God multiplies our "seed" and yields for us a return. But this raises a question: Since when was God our steward, producing a return on our resources? Aren't we His stewards, producing a return on His resources?

What if everything we've learned about sowing and reaping isn't actually God's desire for us? What if He doesn't want you to reap what you've sown? What if He has a different plan? Let us get a little Kingdom perspective and put things in order.

In the coming paragraphs, I'm going to show you:

1. Why our typical perspective of sowing and reaping is so limiting,
2. What God's preferred outcome for your good deeds actually is, and
3. The true source and purpose of worldly riches among Christians.

We'll start with the obvious and broad principles to lay the groundwork and then start talking about money again.

The Divine Exchange that Happened at the Cross...

It begins simply enough: If God wanted you to reap what you have sown, then He never would have sent Jesus to die for you. And yet, *"While we were still sinners, Christ died for us."* (Romans 5:8) How's that for sowing and reaping?

The nature of the New Covenant is that we no longer reap what we have personally sown. Rather, Jesus reaps what we have sown, while we reap what Jesus has sown. Our Lord has forever instituted a divine exchange: Again, Jesus died because HE reaped what YOU have sown; and by grace, He gives you life so that YOU can reap what HE has sown!

In the parable of the Ten Minas, we learn an interesting lesson: The King expects to reap what His servants have sown. And as a result, He — out of His own good will — blessed the faithful servants with an unrelated reward: cities (authority), which should have been His alone to enjoy. (Luke 19:11-27) In verse 21, we read the servant's words: *"You take out what you did not put in and reap what you did not sow."*

Jesus, our gracious King reaps the good and bad from whatever we've sown, and we reap the good and bad from whatever He has sown (thankfully, He has only ever sown good!). Jesus has never sown wickedness; WE have. And yet, He chose to reap the penalty on our behalf.

Romans 6:21-23 (NIV84)

> *What benefit did you reap at that time from the things you are now ashamed of? Those things result in death! But now that you have been set free from sin and have become slaves to God, the benefit you reap leads to holiness, and the result is eternal life. For the wages of sin is death, but the gift of God is eternal life in Christ Jesus our Lord.*

According to this verse, whatever good we now reap is a free gift — not from our own doing. Eternal life is the reward for a righteous life. (Matthew 25:46) And yet, we know, that not a single one of us is righteous. (Romans 3:10.) That's why it's called "the gift of God." We can't earn it. There's nothing we can sow to rightly reap anything good from the Lord. The only way we can possibly have eternal life (or any blessing, for that matter) is if we reap what Jesus has sown. He is the only true "Righteous One." And we who receive Him are made righteous by grace, through faith. (Romans 3:20-26.) Why? Because we are reaping what He has sown.

If you want to reap what you've sown, hell will welcome you. If you want to reap what Jesus has sown, then repent of self-pleasing, and surrender your life to the true King. He'll make you righteous — perfect in God's sight.

Who does the Harvest belong to?

By grace, we are *given* the Spirit of sonship. (Romans 8:15), the right of citizenship. As citizen sons, we benefit from the vast resources of our Father's riches in His Kingdom. (Luke 15:31 and John 16:15) Any blessings we have are by virtue of our relationship with Him rather than our own hard work. A son enjoys the blessings of the Father's household, which only exist because of the Father's hard work. Children may be allowed to help their father in the field, but the responsibility for the field belongs to the father, not his children. The children don't multiply the crop — they just obey their father's direction and enjoy the harvest He orchestrated.

Jesus taught that the way of the Kingdom is for people to reap where they have not sown. Consider what He said about doing the work of the Gospel:

John 4:35-38 (NIV84)

> *Do you not say, 'Four months more and then the harvest'? I tell you, open your eyes and look at the fields! They are ripe for harvest.*

> *Even now the reaper draws his wages, even now he harvests the crop for eternal life, so that the sower and the reaper may be glad together.*

> *Thus the saying 'One sows and another reaps' is true. I sent you to reap what you have not worked for. Others have done the hard work, and you have reaped the benefits of their labor.*

Today, we know that any good thing we reap is a result of the work of Jesus. Even in the context of the above verse, any work of value by previous generations only happened because of what God was doing through them. "*So neither he who plants nor he who waters is anything, but only God, who makes things grow.*" (1 Corinthians 3:7.) We may participate in His work, but He is the only true source and purpose of it all. "*One sows and another reaps.*"

We sow; Jesus reaps.

Jesus sows; we reap.

What about Money as "Seed"?

Let's take a look at Ambassador Paul's letter to the Corinthians:

2 Corinthians 9:6-11

> *Remember this: Whoever sows sparingly will also reap sparingly, and whoever sows generously will also reap generously. Each man should give what he has decided in his heart to give, not reluctantly or under compulsion, for God loves a cheerful giver. And God is able to make all grace abound to you, so that in all things at all times, having all that you need, you will abound in every good work. As it is written:*
>
>> *"He has scattered abroad his gifts to the poor; his righteousness endures forever."*
>
> *Now He who supplies seed to the sower and bread for food will also supply and increase your store of seed and will enlarge the harvest of your righteousness. You will be made rich in every way so that you can be generous on every occasion, and through us your generosity will result in thanksgiving to God.*

If you read this closely, it supports the thesis of this section. If this verse was about receiving a direct turnaround of money for what we've sown, then why does it talk so much about meritless grace?

"God is able to make all grace abound to you"

"He has scattered abroad His gifts to the poor"

"He... supplies seed to the sower and bread for food"

This passage is clear about definitions and sources:

- God supplies the seed.
- God increases the store of seed.
- God makes you "rich in every way" SO THAT you can be generous.

The only "harvest" mentioned here for your benefit is a "harvest *of righteousness.*"

The cause and effect here is clear: God — with His meritless, unearned favor — blesses us with resources we don't deserve. And the purpose is for us to sow generously. If we sow our resources generously for Him, then He will sow His resources generously for us. We sow finances generously, and we reap righteousness generously — not because righteousness is the plant that grows from money but because we have traded places with Jesus and Kingdom righteousness will unlock the keys and doors to much more than just money in your life. He reaps what we sow, and we reap what He sows. We sow worldly goods; He sows His own blood. He reaps our worldly goods (as His people are cared for and His Gospel is spread), and we reap righteousness. Jesus has transformed it from "sowing and reaping" to become "reaping and sowing!" The blessing comes first, and we sow it — not the other way around!

Do you see it?

Under the New Covenant of grace, we no longer give in order to receive. Rather, we receive in order to give. The reason we sow generously is that we want to reap generously — not to reap money, but to reap righteousness. How? Righteousness is what Jesus should be reaping, but He doesn't need it because He is already righteous. Instead He shares His harvest with us. As we sow to please Him, we reap His reward.

Jesus Reaps What You Have Sown

Once the glorious exchange of the cross takes place, we reap what King Jesus has sown, and He reaps what we have sown. Every evil deed we have sown was reaped in the body of our Lord at the crucifixion. Likewise, every good deed we carry out is for His sake. Jesus reaps the benefit. Jesus said that every good deed we perform is done "unto Him."

Matthew 25:34-40 (NIV84)

> *Then the King will say to those on his right, 'Come, you who are blessed by My Father; take your inheritance, the kingdom prepared for you since the creation of the world. For I was hungry and you gave Me something to eat, I was thirsty and you gave Me something to drink, I was a stranger and you invited Me in, I needed clothes and you clothed Me, I was sick and you looked after Me, I was in prison and you came to visit Me.'*

> *Then the righteous will answer Him, 'Lord, when did we see You hungry and feed You, or thirsty and give You something to drink? When did we see You a stranger and invite You in, or needing clothes and clothe You? When did we see You sick or in prison and go to visit You?'*

> *"The King will reply, 'I tell you the truth, whatever you did for one of the least of these brothers of Mine, you did for Me.'*

As Christians, the good deeds we sow are for Christ's benefit. We don't need to sow for our own benefit because Jesus is already actively doing that. Remember, God blesses us out of love and grace — not because we deserve it. Because of sin, we deserve *nothing but death*. Jesus deserves *everything but death*. The heart of the Gospel is that He traded places with us and then rose from the dead, reigning victorious over the sting of sin. (1 Corinthians 15:54-57) Can you see how the Kingdom works though all this?

Psalm 24:1

> ...*The earth is the LORD'S, and the fulness thereof; the world, and they that dwell therein.*

You cannot give anything to the King that is not already His, including yourself!

By you're sowing unto the Kingdom you are acknowledging the headship of the King and sovereignty of the Kingdom which in turn is returned to you in righteousness, which is the passport to access the Kingdom benefits!

Sow to Please the Spirit

Many Christians have the idea that putting money in the church offering plate will result in financial blessing for them. The fact is, it will! But there's more to it than that..

If you're giving for the sake of receiving, then you're living according to the Law rather than according to grace. You're "sowing" in order to fill your bank account rather than "sowing" so that Kingdom might reap the reward. In essence, it's nothing more than dabbling in magic: using spiritual laws to achieve worldly gain. And yet this is where the prosperity gospel has gone astray and we teach this in our churches! May God forgive us. We don't sow for the pleasure of our own reaping. We sow for the Lord's pleasure and for the benefit of the Kingdom!

Galatians 6:8

> *The one who sows to please his sinful nature, from that nature will reap destruction; the one who sows to please the Spirit, from the Spirit will reap eternal life.*

You can sow to please God or you can sow to please yourself. Who would you rather have reap the reward? Jesus said that when we do things for the sake of our own benefit — being seen by men rather than by God — we have received our rewards in full. (Matthew 6:2,5,16.) But if we do things for His benefit — secretly and in intimacy with Him, we receive blessing from the Father. If you want to live according to the law, then you'll receive your reward from the law. Unfortunately, it tramples the cross of Christ.

Giving always results in receiving, but it functions differently under the New Covenant. Under the *Old* Covenant, if you sow riches, you will reap more riches. Everything remains in the natural realm. Under the *New* Covenant, if you sow riches, you reap righteousness — in other words, you reap the benefits of the Kingdom which far exceed the boundaries of earthly money (Mammon). Instead, *He* reaps the riches. Just as the ocean of angels around heaven's throne have declared, "*Worthy is the Lamb, who was slain, to receive power and wealth and wisdom and strength and honor and glory and praise!*" (See Revelation 5:12.)

What use does Jesus have for wealth? What good is it in heaven? In heaven, the streets are paved with gold. This world's wealth is like dirt there! It only makes sense that whatever worldly wealth Jesus may reap is going to be spent during this present age for the sake of His Bride and His lost sheep here on earth. So He freely distributes what He has — either to trustworthy people or to people who He would like to train in stewardship.

As we read in Psalms 24:1, it all belongs to the King.. It's all Gods! Every penny we have belongs to the King. It's *His* seed, which *He* has provided to the sowers; and some of it is "bread," for our own consumption. (2 Corinthians 9:10.) All of it belongs to Him, and none of it belongs to us. We don't reap from it. We sow it. The King reaps the reward. And if we are faithful stewards, He will entrust more to us. Get it?

No longer are we slaves to an impersonal law; now we are favored children of the King who reap the benefits of His limitless, unearned love! And what we receive in this place of relationship is far greater than any financial return: "a harvest of righteousness." The servants who properly stewarded the King's money were placed in charge of cities! All that the Father has is ours.

Under the Old Covenant, we give to receive. Under the New Covenant, we receive to give.

So should you stop giving to churches or nonprofits? By no means! If the Gospel is being multiplied through an organization, then it's a great place to sow seed. You can also give directly to the needy and the widows (there may not be a tax write-off for you, but Jesus will receive His reward). Every gift you give and every good deed you perform is done unto Jesus because He will reap the reward. He alone is worthy to receive ALL the return on your investment. And as He sees that you are faithfully stewarding His resources for His sake, He will know that He can give you more resources to faithfully steward for His sake. Remember, He will "increase your store of seed."

A Higher Principle: Stewardship

Remember, in the Kingdom, we own nothing and the Lord, or the King own everything...We are merely stewards of His earth and resources. So next time you think you are putting $100 in the offering as if you are giving to God, rethink it! You are returning unto Him, a portion of what is already His!

Psalm 24:1

> ...The earth is the LORD'S, and the fulness thereof; the world, and they that dwell therein.

Sometimes God's blessings are a response to faithful stewardship, and sometimes they are simply unearned gifts. The way we handle the unearned gifts is an indicator of how we will handle His investments. If we're constantly sowing for our own sake, then we can't be trusted with any more than the unearned gifts. But if we're constantly sowing for His sake, then we can be trusted with more.

That said, one's riches are not equal to his or her holiness. On the contrary, the most generous givers are the ones who will most generously reap *righteousness*. The only person Jesus ever praised for their giving (at least in the recorded Gospels) was the poor widow who gave 100% of all she had (Mark 12:41-44). Likewise, Paul held up as an example the Macedonian Christians:

1 Corinthians 8:2-4

> *Out of the most severe trial, their overflowing joy and their extreme poverty welled up in rich generosity. For I testify that they gave as much as they were able, and even beyond their ability. Entirely on their own, they urgently pleaded with us for the privilege of sharing in this service to the saints."*

We should never gauge someone's spirituality by how much money they have. The "poorest" person may only be "poor" because they give away all of their million-dollar salary every year. And the "richest" person may only be "rich" because they hoard all of their measly income. Never allow yourself to fall into the trap of judging people based on what they have. And understand that every seed will reap a harvest because

Gen 8:22

> *While the earth remaineth, seedtime and harvest, and cold and heat, and summer and winter, and day and night shall not cease.*

Spiritual Law 5: The Law of Disposition

God chooses what Man despises. We have a habit in the world to place high value on the wrong things; Our King has a practice of setting that straight! After all, He saw me fit for His Kingdom, so to me that is the ultimate reflection of this principle.

> *27 But God hath chosen the foolish things of the world to confound the wise; and God hath chosen the weak things of the world to confound the things which are mighty;*
>
> *28 And base things of the world, and things which are despised, hath God chosen, yea, and things which are not, to bring to nought things that are:*

Matthew 18:10

> *10 Take heed that ye despise not one of these little ones; for I say unto you, That in heaven their angels do always behold the face of my Father which is in heaven.*

Spiritual Law 6: The Law of Mutual Forgiveness

God not only forgives those who forgive others, but with the same measure of your forgiveness. Now that's heavy for us New Testament Christians who come to the Kingdom accept Christ in their hearts and take His forgiveness, which is a free gift by grace, then go and hold others accountable for their sins.

Matthew 6:14-15

14 For if ye forgive men their trespasses, your heavenly Father will also forgive you:

> *15 But if ye forgive not men their trespasses, neither will your Father forgive your trespasses*

Matthew 18:23-25

> *²³ Therefore is the kingdom of heaven likened unto a certain king, which would take account of his servants.*
>
> *²⁴ And when he had begun to reckon, one was brought unto him, which owed him ten thousand talents.*
>
> *²⁵ But forasmuch as he had not to pay, his lord commanded him to be sold, and his wife, and children, and all that he had, and payment to be made.*

Let's clarify this. This is Jesus speaking above.. If it were in your KJB, the letters would be in red. It seems like a contradiction to what we have been taught, because it is. When we come to Christ and dedicate our lives to Him as our Lord, King and Savior, He is faithful and just and forgives us of all unrighteousness and sin. As of this point in time, you are as righteous as you will ever be and all the benefits a=of the Kingdom are opened up to you. This is why we see many new born Christians having all their prayers answered. But then someti9ng happens, we allow sin to creep back in and start holding on to what the King freed you of, and one of these things is forgiveness against others. All the Laws work together.. this is sowing and reaping... If you do not forgive others, how can your Lord forgive you?

Mathew 5:7

> *Blessed are the merciful, for they shall receive mercy."*

So receiving mercy comes to us through our being merciful. That is almost the same as:

Mathew 6:15

> *But if ye forgive not men their trespasses, neither will your Father*
> *forgive your trespasses.*

We receive mercy at the judgment if trusting Christ's mercy has made us merciful. James puts it this way:

James 2:13

> *Judgment [by God] is without mercy to one who has shown no*
> *mercy. Mercy triumphs over judgment.*

Mark 11:25

> *And when ye stand praying, forgive, if ye have ought against*
> *any: that your Father also which is in heaven may forgive you*
> *your trespasses.*

That is, if we show mercy, our judgment will not be condemnation, it will be mercy. If you forgive, you will be forgiven. Citizen of the Kingdom, please hear me; when you hold back forgiveness, compassion or clemency from someone, when you hold a grudge or bitterness towards someone, you restrain yourself from the benefits of the Kingdom. Essentially, you hold yourself in bondage, not the person you have a grudge against.

Someone told me in response to this teaching *"My forgiveness is not predicated on anything because it would then be works and not grace"*.. That is simply incorrect. It is by grace you are given forgiveness and though faith you receive it. Is faith a work? You cannot please God without it. Jesus Himself said to pray for God to *forgive us our trespasses as we forgive those who trespass against us* (Mathew 6:12) then He followed the prayer up and stated plainly in verse 15 *But if ye forgive not men their trespasses, neither will your Father forgive your trespasses.* Reading this in context, it is plain to see that Jesus is speaking to His disciples and predicates it all with the following statement:

Mathew 5:6-20

> ^{6} Let your light so shine before men, that they may see your good works, and glorify your Father which is in heaven.

> ^{17} Think not that I am come to destroy the law, or the prophets: I am not come to destroy, but to fulfil.

> ^{18} For verily I say unto you, Till heaven and earth pass, one jot or one tittle shall in no wise pass from the law, till all be fulfilled.

> ^{19} Whosoever therefore shall break one of these least commandments, and shall teach men so, he shall be called the least in the kingdom of heaven: but whosoever shall do and teach them, the same shall be called great in the kingdom of heaven.

> ^{20} For I say unto you, That except your righteousness shall exceed the righteousness of the scribes and Pharisees, ye shall in no case enter into the kingdom of heaven.

Then our King proceeds to say, ye have heard, but I say.. which means He is laying the Kingdom groundwork for everything going forward... Herein was the Lords Prayer and His closing statements *"if ye forgive not men their trespasses, neither will your Father forgive your trespasses"*. I included this in this section so no man can say that this was before Christ's death and resurrection and does not count... Anyone preaching this is incorrect as it is clear in the context of scripture that this is for you, today. So I reiterate:

Matthew 6:14-15

> *14 For if ye forgive men their trespasses, your heavenly Father will also forgive you:*
>
> *15 But if ye forgive not men their trespasses, neither will your Father forgive your trespasses*

Lastly, let me state that the worst person you can hold unforgiveness against is yourself. This is called condemnation. When you repent of sin and iniquity, your King is faithful and just to forgive you; but many hold themselves in bondage because the devil, the king of darkness wants to keep you in darkness and away from the promises and benefits that forgiveness brings. This robs you of righteousness that is brought by forgiveness and as long as you feel that God did not forgive you for what He said He has, you will restrain yourself from Kingdom access in that area, especially as it relates to law #6 below.

Spiritual Law 7: The Law of Equivalence of Forgiveness and Healing

There is reciprocity between forgiveness and healing. This is a powerful law and principle. Being forgiven means being healed.

Sickness and disease are a curse. They are part of the curse of the fall and part of the curse of the law. The earth remains under a curse because of the fall of man in the garden of Eden, but through Christ, you are redeemed from the curse of the "Law" as we understand from Galatians 3:13 and by the Law of redemption above. Because you are reunited to the Kingdom, you are redeemed from the curse of sickness and disease that came from that initial separation.

I looked for an instance in the walk of Jesus where someone was healed and forgiveness didn't precede it, or vice versa.. I could not find one. So if you have received the forgiveness (the pardon) that the King provided to you in Law 6 above, then you have exchanged your sin for

His righteousness and have every right to healing.. In fact, it would be a violation of spiritual law and principle for sickness to be in your body, so make your demand in faith according to the Law of Faith (Law #2 above) and take your healing as a citizen right!

Corinthians 11:29-30

> *²⁹ For he that eateth and drinketh unworthily, eateth and drinketh damnation to himself, not discerning the Lord's body.*

> *³⁰ For this cause many are weak and sickly among you, and many sleep.*

Matthew 9:5

> *⁵ For whether is easier, to say, Thy sins be forgiven thee; or to say, Arise, and walk?*

Isaiah 33:24

> *²⁴ And the inhabitant shall not say, I am sick: the people that dwell therein shall be forgiven their iniquity.*

Deuteronomy 28:58-61

> *⁵⁸ If thou wilt not observe to do all the words of this law that are written in this book, that thou mayest fear this glorious and fearful name, The Lord Thy God;*

> *⁵⁹ Then the Lord will make thy plagues wonderful, and the plagues of thy seed, even great plagues, and of long continuance, and sore sicknesses, and of long continuance.*

> *⁶⁰ Moreover he will bring upon thee all the diseases of Egypt, which thou wast afraid of; and they shall cleave unto thee.*

⁶¹ Also every sickness, and every plague, which is not written in the book of this law, them will the Lord bring upon thee, until thou be destroyed.

Spiritual Law 8: The Law of Greatness

Plain and simple; converse to the worlds system, in our Kingdom if you want to be great, learn to serve!

Mark 10:43-44

⁴³ But so shall it not be among you: but whosoever will be great among you, shall be your minister:

⁴⁴ And whosoever of you will be the chiefest, shall be servant of all

Spiritual Law 9: The Law of Position

God evaluates people differently than man does. When you are in the Kingdom, it is not about stature, wealth, prestige, who your family is or where you are from.. Remember, even Jesus came from a lowly town called Nazareth.

Matthew 20:16

⁶ So the last shall be first, and the first last: for many be called, but few chosen.

1 Samuel 16:7

⁷ But the Lord said unto Samuel, Look not on his countenance, or on the height of his stature; because I have refused him: for the Lord seeth not as man seeth; for man looketh on the outward appearance, but the Lord looketh on the heart.

Spiritual Law 10: The Law of Life Preservation

In struggling to save our lives we lose them; losing our lives for Jesus' sake, we save them. If you place a higher priority on your life than the Kingdom, you are out of order with the Kingdom.

Matthew 16:25

> *For whosoever will save his life shall lose it: and whosoever will lose his life for my sake shall find it.*

There is a reason Mathew 6:33 states to take no thought of the things of this world, but rather seek first, primary, before anything in your life the Kingdom of God and the righteousness of the King. Your life here is but a vapor according to James. Stop your worrying, prepping and fearing (having faith in) over what the current economy, wars, shortages or anything else will do to you and put the Kingdom first, then you will gain everything else.

Spiritual Law 11: The Law of Living/Dying

Here is another Law that is in opposition to the worlds system..

Galatians 2:20

> *I am crucified with Christ: nevertheless I live; yet not I, but Christ liveth in me: and the life which I now live in the flesh I live by the faith of the Son of God, who loved me, and gave himself for me.*

Romans 6:4-5

> *4 Therefore we are buried with him by baptism into death: that like as Christ was raised up from the dead by the glory of the Father, even so we also should walk in newness of life.*

⁵ For if we have been planted together in the likeness of his death, we shall be also in the likeness of his resurrection:

Spiritual Law 12: The Law of Strength

Similar to giving up your life that you may save it, is the Law of strength..

2 Corinthians 12:9

> *And he said unto me, My grace is sufficient for thee: for my strength is made perfect in weakness. Most gladly therefore will I rather glory in my infirmities, that the power of Christ may rest upon me.*

2 Corinthians 12:10

> *Therefore I take pleasure in infirmities, in reproaches, in necessities, in persecutions, in distresses for Christ's sake: for when I am weak, then am I strong.*

Hebrews 11:34

> *Quenched the violence of fire, escaped the edge of the sword, out of weakness were made strong, waxed valiant in fight, turned to flight the armies of the aliens.*

Joel 3:10

> *Beat your plowshares into swords and your pruning hooks into spears: let the weak say, I am strong.*

Spiritual Law 13: The Law of Victory

Our victory comes from our faith in the finished works of the cross.

1 John 5:4-5

> [4] *For whatsoever is born of God overcometh the world: and this is the victory that overcometh the world, even our faith.*

> [5] *Who is he that overcometh the world, but he that believeth that Jesus is the Son of God?*

Spiritual Law 14: The Law of Priority

God is a God of priority and the Kingdom is a Kingdom of priority and divine order. If you want Kingdom results then operate according to the Kingdom order and priority...

Mathew 6:21

For where your treasure is, there will your heart be also.

Luke 4:8

> *And Jesus answered and said unto him, Get thee behind me, Satan: for it is written, Thou shalt worship the Lord thy God, and Him only shalt thou serve.*

Mathew 6:25-33

> [25] *Therefore I say unto you, <u>Take no thought for your life</u>, what ye shall eat, or what ye shall drink; nor yet for your body, what ye shall put on. Is not the life more than meat, and the body than raiment?*

> [26] *Behold the fowls of the air: for they sow not, neither do they reap, nor gather into barns; yet your heavenly Father feedeth them. Are ye not much better than they?*

[27] *Which of you by taking thought can add one cubit unto his stature?*

28 And why take ye thought for raiment? Consider the lilies of the field, how they grow; they toil not, neither do they spin:

29 And yet I say unto you, That even Solomon in all his glory was not arrayed like one of these.

30 Wherefore, if God so clothe the grass of the field, which to day is, and to morrow is cast into the oven, shall he not much more clothe you, O ye of little faith?

31 Therefore take no thought, saying, What shall we eat? or, What shall we drink? or, Wherewithal shall we be clothed?

32 (For after all these things do the Gentiles seek:) for your heavenly Father knoweth that ye have need of all these things.

33 But seek ye first the kingdom of God, and his righteousness; and all these things shall be added unto you.

OK, lets look at verse 31/32 again... He says Take no thought of these things.. what things? What are you going to eat, drink, wear.. etc.. He says that these things the Gentiles (or the non-Kingdom citizens) seek after. So if you want to be a Kingdom citizen the seek FIRST the Kingdom and the Righteousness of God and then ALL these things will be added unto you... Like so many others, I bet you had this backward?

Let me say to the hoarder and the prepper... If you are doing it because you fear not having it one day, or that you will lack the things you desire.. That is a fear based decision and you are putting the wrong kingdom first... Take no thought! Not if you want to operate in the Kingdom, because when your preps run out, the Kingdom cannot provide for you because you opted to trust in another system first. But, if you put the Kingdom of God first, I promise you that no matter what happens here on earth, God will sustain you and ensure that all those things are added to you at all times. Do you get the priority?

Am I saying do not think ahead or prepare for disaster? Not at all, in fact it is prudent; but keep your priorities straight and make sure it is not done out of fear.

Spiritual Law 15: The Law of Hearing and Believing

Romans 10:13-14

> *For whosoever shall call upon the name of the Lord shall be saved. How then shall they call on him in whom they have not believed? and how shall they believe in him of whom they have not heard? and how shall they hear without a preacher?*

Romans 10:17

So then faith cometh by hearing, and hearing by the word of God.

Exodus 4:31

> *And the people believed: and when they heard that the Lord had visited the children of Israel, and that he had looked upon their affliction, then they bowed their heads and worshipped.*

John 5:24

> *Verily, verily, I say unto you, He that heareth my word, and believeth on him that sent me, hath everlasting life, and shall not come into condemnation; but is passed from death unto life.*

It works in the inverse also...

Luke 8:12

> *Those by the way side are they that hear; then cometh the devil, and taketh away the word out of their hearts, lest they should believe and be saved.*

Spiritual Law 16: The Law of Judgment

This is not too popular with many Christians because of a misunderstanding of Grace, but we shall be judged with the same judgment that we give to others.

Matthew 7:2

> *For with what judgment ye judge, ye shall be judged: and with what measure ye mete, it shall be measured to you again.*

I had a conversation with someone who attempted to explain to me that being that this conversation happened before the cross and resurrection it was non-applicable... Let me show you why that is wrong and very much so applicable today and forever.

Mathew 18:22-35

> *²² Jesus saith unto him, I say not unto thee, Until seven times: but, Until seventy times seven.*
>
> *²³ Therefore is the kingdom of heaven likened unto a certain king, which would take account of his servants.*
>
> *²⁴ And when he had begun to reckon, one was brought unto him, which owed him ten thousand talents.*
>
> *²⁵ But forasmuch as he had not to pay, his lord commanded him to be sold, and his wife, and children, and all that he had, and payment to be made.*
>
> *²⁶ The servant therefore fell down, and worshipped him, saying, Lord, have patience with me, and I will pay thee all.*
>
> *²⁷ Then the lord of that servant was moved with compassion, and loosed him, and forgave him the debt.*

²⁸ But the same servant went out, and found one of his fellowservants, which owed him an hundred pence: and he laid hands on him, and took him by the throat, saying, Pay me that thou owest.

²⁹ And his fellowservant fell down at his feet, and besought him, saying, Have patience with me, and I will pay thee all.

³⁰ And he would not: but went and cast him into prison, till he should pay the debt.

³¹ So when his fellowservants saw what was done, they were very sorry, and came and told unto their lord all that was done.

³² Then his lord, after that he had called him, said unto him, O thou wicked servant, I forgave thee all that debt, because thou desiredst me:

³³ Shouldest not thou also have had compassion on thy fellowservant, even as I had pity on thee?

³⁴ And his lord was wroth, and delivered him to the tormentors, till he should pay all that was due unto him.

³⁵ So likewise shall my heavenly Father do also unto you, if ye from your hearts forgive not every one his brother their trespasses.

My Pastor used to say that the disciples were not asking Jesus how many times they should forgive because they wanted to make sure they were fulfilling the requirement.. they were asking because they wanted to know when they can stop forgiving! But the 70 X 7 is an infinite response!

So by now you should have the understanding of the Kingdom to know that the King never changes .. in fact, he specifically tells us this in Malachi 3:6 – *"For I am the Lord, I change not..."* And if the King does not change, neither does the Kingdom. It is an everlasting Kingdom that cannot change or be altered in its laws, rules, standards or otherwise the entire bible is false and the world will fall apart because God bases everything here on earth, as it is in the eternal Kingdom of heaven.. The King can't change the rules, they are always the same. So when you see Jesus saying at any time. The Kingdom of God/Heaven is likened to, or like, or as... you can take that to the bank that what He is about to say is a forever principle. Now, re-read that last passage again if you need to, then forgive anyone who you may be holding unforgiveness towards because the weight of that is on you.

And while I am here, let me touch upon self forgiveness, because you must also learn to forgive yourself and believe it or not you can hold yourself in contempt with self – unforgiveness. It will hold you back from taking on the righteousness that is freely yours. This is why 1 Corinthians 11 says that if we judge ourselves, we should not be judged.

So judge yourself and forgive others for their sins against your and/or others, and forgive yourself so your King can forgive you. I know that's heavy.. but He is giving us something we do not deserve by forgiving us for all sin from the time of Adam through eternity (even what you haven't done yet!). So freely you receive, freely you should give and do not withhold the power of the cross from anyone. This is an important access lesson if received properly, and a major Key to righteousness.

Spiritual Law 17: The Law of Apostasy

If we serve foreign gods, God will cause us to serve the foreigners who worship these gods. Plain and simple. This was Solomons downfall and sadly we see America going in this same direction..

Judges 2:13-14

> *13 And they forsook the Lord, and served Baal and Ashtaroth.*

14 And the anger of the Lord was hot against Israel, and he delivered them into the hands of spoilers that spoiled them, and he sold them into the hands of their enemies round about, so that they could not any longer stand before their enemies.

Judges 10:6-7

6 And the children of Israel did evil again in the sight of the Lord, and served Baalim, and Ashtaroth, and the gods of Syria, and the gods of Zidon, and the gods of Moab, and the gods of the children of Ammon, and the gods of the Philistines, and forsook the Lord, and served not him.

7 And the anger of the Lord was hot against Israel, and he sold them into the hands of the Philistines, and into the hands of the children of Ammon.

Jeremiah 5:19

And it shall come to pass, when ye shall say, Wherefore doeth the Lord our God all these things unto us? then shalt thou answer them, Like as ye have forsaken me, and served strange gods in your land, so shall ye serve strangers in a land that is not your's.

Spiritual Law 18: The Law of Humility

God exalts those who humble themselves. We live in a promote yourself, put your best foot forward world. Posts of new cars, new clothes, and perfect vacations fill our social media feeds. We stroke our egos by seeking the approval of others. Success coaches teach people how to push your way to the front of the crowd and focus the attention on you.

God's economy works differently. God says if you want to be promoted, humble yourself before your King.

Don't get me wrong. God is not against promotion. God loves to bless and to promote His children. The word "exalt" means to receive a high place of privilege and honor. God honors those who humble themselves before Him. When you humble yourself, you confess your need of Him —humbling yourself before God is confessing that He is your Lord, your King, and you aren't. Humbling yourself is submitting your life, desires, and will to Him. It is offering yourself as a living sacrifice before God and thus, putting the King and the Kingdom first as in Mathew 6:33 that we read earlier.

Too often, we do His job. We exalt ourselves. But when you humble yourself before God, you release God's incredible power to work in your life. God promises to exalt us in due season. That means He will exalt us on His time frame, not ours.

Humbling yourself under the mighty hand of God is allowing God to work in your life. Sometimes, when you feel the pressure of God's hand on you, you resist. You fight back against God's work in your life. But when you release your life into the Kings hands, you open the doors for Him to send His blessings into your life.

> 1 Peter 5:6

> *Humble yourselves therefore under the mighty hand of God, that he may exalt you in due time:*

> James 4:10

> *Humble yourselves in the sight of the Lord, and he shall lift you up.*

Spiritual Law 19: The Law of Restoration

If a thief is found, he shall restore seven-fold what he stole. I love this one because we have a habit of doing warfare as if you are going to make the devil restore what he stole. The law of the Kingdom states that if the thief be found, he must restore seven fold. That means the only requisite on your end is to identify the thief. Once you point him out to the King, he is bound to repay you for all he stole seven fold!

Proverbs 6:31

> *But if he (the thief) be found, he shall restore sevenfold; he shall give all the substance of his house.*

One important note and thing to consider is that many times there is no thief. We blame the devil for consequences of our own decisions as a way to negate responsibility. So before blaming the devil for something before the King, make sure that he is the thief and that whatever you lost was not just a consequence of your bad decisions somewhere down the line. Remember, if you soe corruption to the flesh you will reap corruption so if you have a mouth full of cavities because you ate too much candy, did drugs or do not brush your teeth, it's not the devil, it's not a curse or anything else.. it was you! But here is the good news, once you forsake that decision and turn from it (maybe start flossing!) and repent, your king will forgive your transgression even against yourself and position you for healing!

Spiritual Law 20: The Law of Defilement

Evil words & thoughts which come from the heart defile the person.

There is a reason Proverbs tells us to guard your heart with all diligence because out of it (your heart) flow the issues or the parameters of your life. This is also the same reason that we as Christians will be judged for every idle word spoken (Matthew 12:36).

Mathew 15:18-20

> *¹⁸ But those things which proceed out of the mouth come forth from the heart; and they defile the man.*

> *¹⁹ For out of the heart proceed evil thoughts, murders, adulteries, fornications, thefts, false witness, blasphemies:*

> *²⁰ These are the things which defile a man: but to eat with unwashen hands defileth not a man.*

When The King creates, He speaks... when you as a citizen of the Kingdom create, exercise dominion or rule on earth; we speak with the authority of the King. Your words are power capsules, and to speak wrongful, hurtful or even empty words is a violation of the Kingdom.

Spiritual Law 21: The Law of Multiplication

Multiplication takes place by thanksgiving

2 Corinthians 9:12

> *For the administration of this service not only supplieth the want of the saints, but is abundant also by many thanksgivings unto God;*

John 6:11

> *And Jesus took the loaves; and when he had given thanks, he distributed to the disciples, and the disciples to them that were set down; and likewise of the fishes as much as they would.*

Jeremiah 30:19

> *'From them will proceed thanksgiving*
>
> *And the voice of those who celebrate;*
>
> *And I will multiply them and they will not be diminished;*
>
> *I will also honor them and they will not be insignificant.*

Matthew 15:36

> *And he took the seven loaves and the fishes, and gave thanks, and brake them, and gave to his disciples, and the disciples to the multitude.*

If you want to see multiplication in your life, show the King your thankfulness for what you have.

As I close this chapter, I want you to note that it cannot be said that there is a shortage of scriptural substantiation for everything I have written. The next few chapters will begin to weave everything together into the foundation and fortress of not only understanding but will be the catalyst that will propel you into thinking, acting, walking, talking and having dominion over every circumstance on this earth for the purpose of expanding the Kingdom of God in your life and around you.

VIII

Kingdom Righteousness

In studying out Kingdom Righteousness, I realize that there while there is only one form of righteousness, there are two areas of righteousness that we must understand in order to gain the fullness of the Gospel. One is an imputed righteousness that comes from accepting Jesus as Lord and King, and the other is a practical that comes from walking in obedience to the Kingdom laws stated in the last chapter. There is also a (third) righteousness that is described in the Old Testament that commanded your obedience to become righteous. This was done away with on the cross and replaced with the imputed righteousness of Christ that I will discuss first.

I want to get this straight into your spirit because many have a hard time with it... As a direct characteristic of the King.. God is Righteous. Just as God is Love... It is an attribute of the King, so to know God, is to know Love, or for that matter to know your King is to know righteousness. What that means is that when you accept Jesus Christ as your Lord and King, His righteous virtue has come upon and in you. It is imputed and imparted. You did nothing to earn it, and you can do nothing to get more of it. 100% of the Kings virtue is upon you if you will receive it. This is key to your salvation and Kingdom citizenship.

For the righteous Lord loveth righteousness; his countenance doth behold the upright.

The imputed righteousness is necessary to enter into citizenship in the Kingdom of God (salvation), and the second will reveal a deeper understanding of your authority in the Kingdom and here on earth. I find that most Christians, or citizens as we will now refer to ourselves, stop their understanding at the salvation benevolence and never dig deeper to the fullness of it. This is why:

Matthew 6:33 says

> But <u>*seek ye first the kingdom of God, and His righteousness*</u>; and *all these things shall be added unto you.*

God wants us to seek God's Kingdom *and His righteousness*. There is a promise that <u>if we do that, then</u> all things will be added (given) to us.

Ignorance will cost you. In all areas of life; you will pay more for what you do not know than what you do. What does that mean? It means that many people think they have all the knowledge they need in an area and never seek it our further.. Never dive in to get the fullest and as a result, never realize and obtain the benefits that that area would have provided to them if they just knew the key to open the right door.

Hosea 4:6

> *My people are destroyed for lack of knowledge:*

You can be a citizen of the USA and never obtain the many benefits available to you because you didn't know they were available. You thought you knew it all.. or you were comfortable getting by as you are... Whatever the reason is; but then many citizens get upset when a new immigrant comes and is taught the system and has benefits handed him/her that you didn't. They were simply taught the system that you didn't take the time to learn yourself.

So what does it mean to seek His Kingdom and His righteousness? I can write another book just on this subject and its vastness, so understand that there is much more than what is here, so I encourage you to study, and as Jesus puts it, seek His righteousness at a deeper level. I promise it will unlock areas of the Kingdom for you that you never imagined!

Let's talk about the first form of Imputed Righteousness:

In *Romans*, Paul stresses the *"righteousness of God"* revealed in the gospel, the *"power of God for salvation to everyone who believes."* And it is proclaimed throughout the earth to *"Jew and Greek"* alike. By the *"righteousness of God,"* he means *HIS "righteousness,"* God's faithfulness to provide salvation for His wayward creatures.

The structure of the clause, *"righteousness of God,"* must be given its full weight. Like the "Love of God" or the *"goodness of God"* and the *"mercy of God,"* it refers to that which belongs to Him, to something that defines who and what God is. As I said, it is a characteristic or attribute of the King Himself. And His *"righteousness"* is found in and demonstrated by His tangible acts on behalf of His children.

The second and third chapters of *Romans* present the gospel as the *Great Leveler*. Both Jews and Gentiles have fallen short of the righteousness of God, therefore, both stand under His *"just sentence."* Consequently, short of divine intervention, Jews and Gentiles alike are destined for *"wrath."*

All men and women are *"without excuse"* because all have sinned. No one is in a proper state to judge others. Regardless of ethnicity, whether *"within the law"* or *"apart from the law,"* all men and women are doomed to experience His *"wrath"* without His redemption.

Romans 2:5-11

> *After your hardness and impenitent heart treasure up for your-*
> *self wrath in the day of wrath and revelation of the righteous*
> *judgment of <u>God,who will render to every man according to his*
> *works;</u>to them that by patience in well-doing seek for glory and*
> *honor and incorruption, everlasting life;but to them that are fac-*
> *tious and obey not the truth, but obey unrighteousness, wrath and*
> *indignation, tribulation and anguish upon every soul of man*
> *that works evil, of the Jew first, and also of the Greek;but glory and*
> *honor and peace to every man that works good, to the Jew first,*
> *and also to the Greek:for there is no respect of persons with God.*

"*<u>God will render to each one according to his works</u>.*" Paul emphasizes the future aspect of His "*wrath.*" It will be unleashed on "*the day when God judges the secrets of men...through Christ Jesus.*" Elsewhere, Paul links this "*day of wrath*" to the moment when Jesus arrives from heaven - the "*Day of the Lord*" - (1 Thessalonians 1:10, 2 Thessalonians 1:5-10).

Next, Paul demonstrates that "*both Jews and Greeks are under sin*" - "*<u>All have sinned and lack the glory of God</u>*" - Therefore, men and women are *NOT* set right with God "*<u>from the works of the Law</u>.*" Instead, the Law "*exposes sin*" for what it is – the *trespass* of God's righteous require-ments - (Romans 3:9-18, 3:23).

But mercifully, the "*<u>righteousness of God</u>*" is being revealed through the proclamation of the gospel, "*<u>through the faith of Jesus Christ for all who believe.</u>*"

In him, God declares all who believe "*righteous by His grace, through the redemption that is in Christ Jesus,*" and all this is provided *<u>apart from the works required by the law</u>*- (Romans 3:22-24).

This has been done "*<u>with a view to a showing forth of His righteousness in the present season</u>.*" In Paul's teaching, the stress falls on the *<u>present</u>*

reality of the *"righteousness of God,"* and this is *demonstrated in the proclamation of the gospel to all nations,* clear evidence of His faithfulness to redeem all men who respond in faith to the message - (Romans 1:16-18, 3:19-30).

Thus, the *faithfulness of God* is unveiled in the *here-and-now* whenever He declares men and women to be in right-standing before Him through the *"faith of Jesus Christ"* and their faithful response to the gospel. The provision of salvation in Christ *demonstrates the righteousness of God*.

God's Kingdom is righteousness and peace and joy in the Holy Spirit.

Romans 14:17-18

> *For the kingdom of God is not eating and drinking, but righteousness and peace and joy in the Holy Spirit. For he who in this way serves Christ is acceptable to God and approved by men.*

In what way do we serve Christ to be acceptable to God and approved by men? Through righteousness and peace and joy in the Holy Spirit.

I said above that it is not a righteousness that comes from our own efforts (self-righteousness) and it is a characteristic of the King Himself. So where does this righteousness in us come from? Along with an abundance of grace, it is a free gift of God through Jesus Christ.

Romans 5:17

> *For if by the transgression of the one, death reigned through the one, much more those who receive the abundance of grace and of the gift of righteousness will reign in life through the One, Jesus Christ.*

Adam sinned and because of that sin, every man sinned and inherited death. But because of Jesus, even though He never sinned, He (Jesus) became sin for us and died on the cross. In doing so <u>we were made</u> righteous.

Because of Jesus' sacrifice, we are now given an abundance of grace and the free gift of righteousness (being in right standing with God).

2 Corinthians 5:21

> *He made Him (Jesus) who knew no sin to be sin on our behalf, so that we might become the righteousness of God in Him.*

So what, or I should say, who is God's righteousness?

We who believe in Jesus are the righteousness of God. When you become a citizen of the Kingdom, you take on the attributes of the King and the Kingdom. Let me recapitulate it differently so you get it.. When we seek the kingdom of God and His righteousness we need to understand and believe that the kingdom of God is itself righteousness and that we are the righteousness of God in Christ Jesus. We are God's Righteousness.

Did you get that? You are the righteousness of God in Christ Jesus, you are God's righteousness.

So if I am the righteousness of God and it is not righteousness from my own actions or efforts (self-righteousness), what about the Ten Commandments (the law)?

Simple! As I said in the opening of the chapter, the imputed righteousness of Jesus your King has done away with that requisite. The righteousness of God has manifested apart from the law (the Ten Commandments). Even though the law and the Prophets testified about the righteousness of God, they could never produce righteousness. It was only Jesus' obedience at the cross that redeemed us. It is a free gift of God's grace and it is only by faith in the truth of Jesus' finished work at the cross that we are justified and not the works of the law.

Galatians 2:16

> *Nevertheless knowing that a man is not justified by the works of the Law but through faith in Christ Jesus, even we have believed in Christ Jesus, so that we may be justified by faith in Christ and not by the works of the Law; since by the works of the Law no flesh will be justified.*

The law has nothing to do with the righteousness of God. Because no one has ever kept the law complete and therefore we all have sinned, we can only become the righteousness of God through faith in Jesus Christ when we believe it and become citizens of the Kingdom of God.

Romans 3:21-23

> *But now apart from the Law the righteousness of God has been manifested, being witnessed by the Law and the Prophets, even the righteousness of God through faith in Jesus Christ for all those who believe; for there is no distinction; for all have sinned and fall short of the glory of God, being justified as a gift by His grace through the redemption which is in Christ Jesus;*

Seeking Gods Kingdom and His righteousness is us believing that we are made right by faith, believing that all of our sins have been dealt with and there is nothing that we did, have to do, or can do to deserve it. When we receive Jesus and (believe in His finished work) we are already made righteous (in right standing with God).

This is Good News, the gospel. The good news is, that we are the righteousness of God and all things in salvation (everything) will be added to us. The power of God for our salvation is in the gospel. It is for everyone that believes. The reason is, that in the gospel the righteousness of God is revealed from faith to faith. This faith gives us the power to live right.

Romans 1:16-17

> *For I am not ashamed of the gospel, for it is the power of God for salvation to everyone who believes, to the Jew first and also to the Greek. For in it the righteousness of God is revealed from faith to faith; as it is written, "BUT THE RIGHTEOUS man SHALL LIVE BY FAITH."*

Jesus Christ and His finished work are the Master key to the Kingdom of God we must seek. We are the righteousness of God in Christ Jesus. When we believe in this we are righteous men by faith. In this, being the righteousness of God in Christ Jesus all things will be added to us.

Luke 17:20-21

> *Now having been questioned by the Pharisees as to when the kingdom of God was coming, He (Jesus) answered them and said, "The kingdom of God is not coming with signs to be observed; nor will they say, 'Look, here it is!' or, 'There it is!' For behold, the kingdom of God is in your midst."*

Stop seeking here or there. Stop worrying about your life. Stop trying to become good enough to deserve what God has already freely given. Start seeking the King and His finished work. Start believing that you are already right with God by His grace because of the finished work of Jesus at the cross. Confess it with your mouth. I am the righteousness of God in Christ Jesus. Now believe it in your heart.

Philippians 3.8-9

> *Indeed, I count everything as loss because of the surpassing worth of knowing Christ Jesus my Lord. For his sake I have suffered the loss of all things and count them as rubbish, in order that I may gain Christ and be found in him, not having a righteousness of my own that comes from the law, but that which comes through faith in Christ, the righteousness from God that depends on faith.*

There is also what I will call a real-world righteousness that has nothing to do with either of the two, but worth mentioning. This is simply doing what is right. It is when Christians practice their position. It is trusting God, acting with discipline, building skill, and living in alignment with God's standards. Scripture repeatedly admonishes us to pursue what is right. The book of Proverbs focuses on practical righteousness. It is a library of real-world things we should do and things we should not do. It provides the people of God with instruction on how to be wise, insightful, and skillful in life. It is a guide for doing what is right and practicing your position in Christ. What is the downside for not following in these subset rules? Missing out on the benefits that following them would bring.

Proverbs 11.4-6

> *Riches do not profit in the day of wrath, but righteousness delivers from death. The righteousness of the blameless keeps his way straight, but the wicked falls by his own wickedness. The righteousness of the upright delivers them, but the treacherous are taken captive by their lust.*

1 Timothy 6.11

> *But you, O man of God, flee these things and pursue righteousness, godliness, faith, love, patience, gentleness.*

Ephesians 4.1

> *Walk in a manner worthy of the calling to which you have been called.*

1 Peter 1.14-16

> *As obedient children, do not be conformed to the passions of your former ignorance, but as he who called you is holy, you also be holy in all your conduct, since it is written, 'You shall be holy, for I am holy.*

Trust God, do the work, pursue what is right, gain wisdom.

Now, the other righteousness I mentioned is a practical righteousness. This involves following a set of principles that are set in motion to achieve a certain end. These principles are also called laws. Do not confuse it with the law and the commandments that was done away with, because these laws are principles that the King, the Lord Himself has established to work forever regardless of where you are in time and space. These principles, as we will later even call them *"Keys"* will open doors for you in the Kingdom that you would not have otherwise opened unless you knew the principle or operated according to it.

Many times, dare I say, that we see people who are not even citizens are taking advantage of these keys simply because they understand their operational value. The reason they can do this is because they are laws and principles, and the very nature of a law is that it works every time, no matter what. And even though they can do this, they will never achieve the fullness of it as you would as a citizen of the Kingdom that only comes with the imparted righteousness of receiving the King by faith.

I was going to write the section on the laws after this one, but I want to create a climatic culmination of all the information contained in this book; so if you need to go back and re-read a section, please do!

Accordingly, when you are standing upright as a citizen of the Kingdom, blameless before your King because of your imputed righteousness, you have access to all the keys of the Kingdom and any door you knock on can be opened to you... I will elaborate on this point more later in the section on taking the Keys. I guarantee you that no matter what you are seeking in life, if it is within the Kingdom, you WILL have total access and use by the time were putting this together.. so read on.

IX

Kingdom Authority

Understanding your authority is paramount to your Kingdom operation on this earth. We have been subservient to the worlds system so long that we have a hard time even comprehending the power and authority the King bestowed on us.

Luke 10:19

> *Behold, I give unto you power to tread on serpents and scorpions, and over all the power of the enemy: and nothing shall by any means hurt you.*

A police officer weighing 160 pounds may effectively stand in front of a tanker truck with an uplifted hand say, "Stop, in the name of the law." Now what does he stop that truck with – his own power? No. Authority. The police officer certainly couldn't stop any vehicle with his physical force. He is appealing to an authority greater than himself — the law — to back him up.

Your authority over Satan is the same way. Jesus said, "*I give you authority over all the power of the enemy.*"

Who is physically stronger, you or Satan? Satan. You cannot overcome him with your natural strength. But your authority does not rest in your strength. Who has more authority, you or Satan? You. Jesus said,

"I give you authority over <u>all</u> the power of the enemy." That's the reason the Bible says, "Resist the devil and he will flee from you." Not because you're stronger, but because Jesus is stronger.

You can overcome Satan though your Kingdom Authority given from God. And you have His authority as citizen of the Kingdom and son/daughter of the King to overcome every attack of Satan.

But here's the rub: Americans were never too fond of kingdom monarchies, especially since King George decided that colonies must drink tea and pay taxes without the representation. This is a challenge for the western church because our country was founded on a revolution, and this causes rebellion to authority to be in our roots and culture to the point of it being a stronghold, that most do not even know they carry. So we grow up not trusting authority and always wanting to be free from any form of leadership or covering. America the beautiful, land of the free.

> *Then said Jesus to those Jews which believed on him, If ye continue in my word, then are ye my disciples indeed;*

<u>*And ye shall know the truth, and the truth shall make you free.*</u>

So Jesus was saying to the Jews who had believed Him, if you live under My authority, then you are my disciple and then you will know the truth, and that truth will set you free! So in the Kingdom, the path to freedom is putting yourself under authority!

Romans 13:1-3

> *Let every soul be subject unto the higher powers. For there is no power but of God: the powers that be are ordained of God.*
>
> *² Whosoever therefore resisteth the power, resisteth the ordinance of God: and they that resist shall receive to themselves damnation.*

Remember the Centurion soldier in Matthew 8:8-9? He told Jesus "...speak the word only, and my servant shall be healed. For I am a man under authority, having soldiers under me: and I say to this man, Go, and he goeth; and to another, Come, and he cometh; and to my servant, Do this, and he doeth it..." Jesus was amazed and said that he has not seen such great faith!

Mark 1:27

> *And they were all amazed, insomuch that they questioned among themselves, saying, What thing is this? what new doctrine is this? for with authority commandeth he even the unclean spirits, and they do obey him.*

Even the devil and demons understand and have to respect authorized power!

What do I mean by "authorized power"? It is the power that Jesus gives to an individual to operate in all the attributes and benefits of the Kingdom of God. He sent His Spirit to dwell in you, as a Governor, permitting you to now have the SAME POWER that raised Christ from the dead, to also dwell in you! For what? So He can give you goose bumps and make you feel good? No!

1 John 3:8

> *"... For this purpose the Son of God was manifested, that he might destroy the works of the devil."*

Remember, it's about restoration to Gods original plan of dominion so that we can rule and reign here on earth and expand the Kingdom of God until the whole earth is filled with His Glory!

Lets go deeper...

Jesus gave the disciples the authority, right here..

Matthew 16:18-20

> *18 And I say also unto thee, That thou art Peter, and upon this rock I will build my church; and the gates of hell shall not prevail against it.*
>
> *19 And I will give unto thee the keys of the kingdom of heaven: and whatsoever thou shalt bind on earth shall be bound in heaven: and whatsoever thou shalt loose on earth shall be loosed in heaven.*

20 Then charged he his disciples that they should tell no man that he was Jesus the Christ.

We will go more into the Keys later, but I want you to see that here Jesus gives authority to bind and to loose.. whatsoever you bind on earth shall be bound in heaven: and whatsoever you loose on earth shall be loosed in heaven. In other words, make earth like heaven and here's the authority to do so... The Authority was not coupled with the Power until Pentecost where the Holy Spirit came and endowed them with Power from on High..

You as a believer today have the Power and Authority though Jesus Christ the King and the indwelling of the Governor (Holy Spirit) Himself and it is your task, your only task to make earth like heaven. What does that look like? Remember Jesus said to pray this way...

Mathew 6:10-13

> *After this manner therefore pray ye: Our Father which art in heaven, Hallowed be thy name.*
>
> **Thy kingdom come, Thy will be done in earth, as it is in heaven.**

Give us this day our daily bread. And forgive us our debts, as we forgive our debtors.

And lead us not into temptation, but deliver us from evil:

For thine is the kingdom, and the power, and the glory, for ever. *Amen.*

Did you see that now? *Thy kingdom come, Thy will be done in earth, as it is in heaven..* Here is the thesis, or the purpose of the prayer.. That Gods Kingdom come and His will be done on earth, as it already is, in heaven. Then He wraps it up and reiterates it with saying *For thine is the kingdom, and the power, and the glory, for ever ..* For Gods is the Kingdom, and His is the Power and His is the Glory! That's also the progression of the Kingdom here on earth.. First Kingdom understanding, then Power, then Glory!

So He's given YOU the authority and the power back to have dominion over the earth and subdue it, and the command is to be fruitful and multiply what He has given you. You are a citizen of Gods Kingdom and your commission is to honor and expand the Kingdom throughout the earth.

Remember this because it is vital to exercising your authority, that it takes faith to walk in it. The Centurion soldier equated spoke of being under authority and understood authority and Jesus called it faith.. in fact, He called it great faith! So you speak and act in authority, though faith. You can do this because you have the confidence that your King loves you, because He cares about His Kingdom, and there is nothing He will not do for those He loves.

Remember, the disciples failed to truly trust and have faith in King Jesus while He was here on earth. He made that plain to them:

Matthew 17:14-20

> *And when they had come to the multitude, a man came to Him, kneeling down to Him and saying, "Lord, have mercy on my son, for he is an epileptic and suffers severely; for he often falls into the fire and often into the water. So I brought him to Your disciples, but they could not cure him.*
>
> *Then Jesus answered and said, "O faithless and perverse generation, how long shall I be with you? How long shall I bear with you? Bring him here to Me." And Jesus rebuked the demon, and it came out of him; and the child was cured from that very hour.*
>
> *Then the disciples came to Jesus privately and said, "Why could we not cast it out?"*
>
> *So Jesus said to them, "Because of your unbelief; for assuredly, I say to you, if you have faith as a mustard seed, you will say to this mountain, 'Move from here to there,' and it will move; and nothing will be impossible for you."*

So we see here that a lack of faith led to a lack of authority. But a small amount of faith can move a mountain if need be.. Literally, because it must obey you!

These Words of King Jesus say it all:

John 14:12-17 NLT

> *I tell you the truth, anyone who believes in Me will do the same works I have done, and even greater works, because I am going to be with the Father.*

You can ask for anything in My name, and I will do it, so that the Son can bring glory to the Father. Yes, ask Me for anything in My name, and I will do it!

If you love me, obey My commandments (That means stay under the Authority of the Kingdom). And I will ask the Father, and He will give you another Advocate, who will never leave you. He is the Holy Spirit, who leads into all truth. The world cannot receive Him, because it isn't looking for Him and doesn't recognize Him. But you know Him, because He lives with you now and later will be in you."

(Read that again!)

I want you to live an abundant life in the Kingdom of God with all the power and authority that is available to its citizens! It is all for His glory!

Philippians 2:13 NLT

For God is working in you, giving you the desire and the power to do what pleases Him.

Ephesians 3:20-21AMP

Now to Him (our King) who is able to [carry out His purpose and] do superabundantly more than all that we dare ask or think [infinitely beyond our greatest prayers, hopes, or dreams], according to His power that is at work within us (Our Holy Spirit – Governor),

to Him be the glory in the church (His Government) and in Christ Jesus throughout all generations forever and ever. Amen.

In Luke 10:19 Jesus told us,

> Behold, **I give you the authority** to trample on serpents and scorpions, and over all the power of the enemy, and nothing shall by any means hurt you.

The authority that Jesus is talking about in Luke 10:19 is not brute force power. It's delegated power, much like that policeman possesses. When that policeman steps out in front of traffic and holds up his hand to stop it, he's not stopping cars and trucks with his own brute strength – he's stopping them with the delegated authority that comes from wearing the uniform. He's backed by the law. Well your King is delegating His Power to you, His Ambassador and there is nothing that can be done to stop it. In fact, you stop any obstacle in its tracks with your authority.

That's the authority you have in Christ your King. You're not stopping the forces of darkness (sickness, fear, evil, lack) with your own strength – you're stopping them with the delegated authority given to you by God in Christ. You're backed by all the Power of God.

How amazing is that? God Almighty, the Lord, the King of kings Himself is the Power behind your authority!

Ephesians 6:10 says,

> *Be strong in the Lord and the power of HIS might.*

That means you can step out in front of the devil, hold up your hand and say no, backed by the power of God's might.

Do you realize that because of the Authority Jesus gave you, you are a joint heir with Him? You share that authority like Joseph ruled Egypt! The door to exercising that authority in Christ hinges on Ephesians 1:20 and Ephesians 2:6, the verses that say we are seated with God in

Christ. I encourage you to meditate on those until you fully grasp the revelation that you are seated with Him, and *you* are the one He moves through. You are his empowered Ambassador here on earth!

Then when adversity arises, use your authority by speaking out what His Word says, using the Name of Jesus. For example, you could say, "Sickness, I command you to leave my body in Jesus' Name according to 1 Peter 2:24 – by His stripes I am healed!" The authority is in the name.

It's like using the name of the President of the United States – that name can get things done. It's the same in the spirit realm, except that the Name of Jesus is higher – carries more weight -- than *any other name* (Philippians 2:9). You are literally using the name of the King of the Kingdom - Think about that! When you use the Name of Jesus, believing that you're seated with Him at the right hand of God, you are backed by all the power in heaven! Every knee must bow to that Name (Philippians 2:10).

Jesus made it very clear that His Name is the key to all authority:

John 14:13-14

> *Whatever you ask in My name, that I will do, that the Father may be glorified in the Son. If you ask anything in My name, I will do it*

In Acts 3 when Peter & John encountered a lame man at the Gate Beautiful, they said, *"In the Name of Jesus, rise up and walk"* and he did! It wasn't their own anointing or power that raised the man – it was the authority in the Name of Jesus.

That same authority belongs to us – using the Name of Jesus Christ Lord of Lords and King of Kings is how we use it!

X

Ambassadors of the Kingdom

Before Jesus returned to Heaven, He said to His followers:

Luke 22:29

> *And I appoint unto you a kingdom, as my Father hath appointed unto me.*

The Kingdom God gave Jesus was passed on by Jesus to His disciples and we as citizens are privileged to be part of this eternal empire. But God chooses for purpose, not just privilege. Jesus left His followers with a responsibility of extending the Kingdom of God throughout the world. They were to be Ambassadors of the Kingdom.

An ambassador is a representative sent by one kingdom to represent and transact business in another. He is a messenger and authorized agent of the kingdom he represents. Paul said:

II Corinthians 5:20

> *We are ambassadors for Christ.*

We are the ambassadors sent by the King to represent and transact the business of the Kingdom of God in the kingdoms of the world.

Our assignment as ambassadors of the Kingdom is a lifetime commitment. Once we have accepted this commission, we cannot look back:

Luke 9:62

> *And Jesus said unto him, No man, having put his hand to the plough, and looking back, is fit for the Kingdom of God.*

As ambassadors, we are to be witnesses for the Kingdom of God. A witness is someone who can testify and present evidence of something experienced first hand. He is one who personally sees, observes, experiences, and produces proof of what he has experienced. Jesus said to His disciples:

John 15:27

> *And ye also shall bear witness, because ye have been with me from the beginning.*

The witness of the ambassadors of the Kingdom was to extend throughout the earth:

Acts 1:8

> *But ye shall receive power after that the Holy Ghost is come upon you: and ye shall be witnesses unto me both in Jerusalem, and in all Judaea, and in Samaria, and unto the uttermost part of the earth.*

If you have ever seen a diplomat or ambassador of another country acting on behalf of his/her country, you will note that they speak directly on behalf of the leader of the country without having to consult them for every decision or word spoken. They do this with authority even to the point of discussing and enforcing international negotiations and policies. They have been authorized and "deputized" by their country's leader. What's important to recognize is that they know the laws of their country, they know the goals, objectives and ideologies of their country, and more importantly, they know the heart, the will and the mind of their leader for whom they speak.

Mathew 18:18-20

> *¹⁸ And Jesus came and spake unto them, saying, All power is given unto me in heaven and in earth.*
>
> *¹⁹ Go ye therefore, and teach all nations, baptizing them in the name of the Father, and of the Son, and of the Holy Ghost:*
>
> *²⁰ Teaching them to observe all things whatsoever I have commanded you: and, lo, I am with you always, even unto the end of the world. Amen.*

He is telling them/us to go, and to go be His witness in the Name of the Father, Son and Holy Spirit... Do you get that? The King just branded His Name on you and appointed you as His ambassador.

1 John 3:8

> *He that committeth sin is of the devil; for the devil sinneth from the beginning. For this purpose the Son of God was manifested, that he might destroy the works of the devil.*

Mathew 4:17

> *From that time Jesus began to preach, and to say, Repent: for the kingdom of heaven is at hand.*

Everywhere Jesus went, He proclaimed the Kingdom and signs flowed Him. He wasn't trying to do miracles, He was simply displaying the Kingdom! So now you are appointed as an Ambassador in the Name and authority of the King, empowered by His Governor, the Holy Spirit and with a mission to teach all nations... Teach them what? About the King and His Kingdom! About your restored place in the Kingdom, about how to have dominion, how to subdue the earth and have dominion over it and how to expand and multiply what is in the Kingdom throughout all the earth until the knowledge of the Glory of the Lord fills the earth as the waters cover the sea!

XI

Kingdom Culture

Culture encompasses many things. Once you understand the culture of a people, you understand the people. Everything that makes a nation a nation and a people a people is wrapped up in their culture.

As we have already seen, for example, every country has land— territory.

Without land there is no country. Historically, the land a people inhabits significantly influences the culture they develop. Desert dwellers, for instance, are unlikely to develop a maritime culture unless they live along the coast. Their culture will reflect the arid environment in which they live.

A second key component of every country is language.

A country is not a country unless it has one major language. Many nations of the world have numerous sublanguages and dialects. But every nation always decides on one major language because language identifies you as a country. Language is the key to unity. It is also a key factor in a nation's culture.

Again, as we saw earlier, all countries have laws. Every nation draws up a body of laws that everyone must obey to ensure peace, order, and security for the citizens. Without law there is no country because the absence of law leads to chaos, and you can't run a country or maintain a stable government on chaos. The laws of a nation reflect the culture of that nation and vice versa. Culture and law each affect the other. Every nation also utilizes specific and unique symbols to represent it and to help inspire unity, patriotism, loyalty, pride of nation, and a strong sense of national identity. The most familiar symbol of any nation is, of course, its flag. A nation's flag symbolizes its history, the sacrifices, suffering, and triumphs of its people, and what the people have constituted themselves to be.

All of these things relate also to culture. Few national symbols are more powerful than the flag. Another element that all nations share in common is a constitution which we know that a constitution is a contract between the people and their government. In many ways a constitution is a cultural document because it contains in codified form the laws, ideals, and values of the people (or of the king, depending on who wrote it).

Furthermore, all nations have a moral code. A nation's moral code embodies the moral

standards under which the people have agreed to live and by which they have chosen to govern themselves. In most cases, a moral code consists of both written and unwritten standards. The written standards are expressed through laws and statutes while the unwritten standards are transmitted primarily through traditions, customs, and culture.

Respect other people's property; do not bear false witness in court; do not steal; do not murder; do not commit adultery—all of these are part of the moral code in virtually every nation and government on earth. A seventh common characteristic of all countries is shared values. In order to have a country that runs effectively, the people must share the same values in common. The people as a whole must agree that they all value the same thing, such as life or peace or freedom.

Every nation also develops its own customs. Customs derive from a nation's shared values. A custom is a customary way of doing something, a behavioral pattern that is not only commonly accepted but also expected. Earlier in the book I told you about my Italian Brooklyn neighborhood and the customs of our small culture there and then. Overall though, customs generally are consistent throughout a nation, although there are many regional variations. Quite often a nation's customs are so distinctive that they become a point of identification for that nation, such as certain traditional manners of dress or kinds of foods.

Finally, there are social norms. These are similar to customs but have greater force and authority within society. Social norms are standards of speech, thought, and behavior that are accepted by the wide majority of the people as right and proper. Violate a custom and you may be thought eccentric; violate a social norm and you risk being ostracized. All of these together—land, language, laws, symbols, constitution, moral code, shared values, customs, and social norms—comprise what we call culture.

What is Culture?

culture

noun

cul·ture | \ ˈkəl-chər \

Definition of *culture*

1a: the customary beliefs, social forms, and material traits of a racial, religious, or social group *also* : the characteristic features of everyday existence (such as diversions or a way of life) shared by people in a place or time popular *culture* Southern *culture*

b: the set of shared attitudes, values, goals, and practices that characterizes an institution or organization

So what is culture specifically? Simply stated, we all come to think like the environment we grow up in. Our intellectual interaction with our environment literally produces a way of thinking in us that becomes our way of life, and so we become trained in our culture.

None of us are born with a culture. We are born into a culture, but we are not born with a culture. Culture may also be defined as the integrated pattern of human knowledge, belief, and behavior that depends upon man's capacity for learning and transmitting knowledge to succeeding generations. From a sociological perspective, culture is the customary beliefs, social forms, and material traits of a racial, religious, or social group.

Just like when you were in school and did experiments in a petri dish, each individual one was called a culture. Well, each of us arrived on earth in a prepared medium, our own petri dish if you will —the country and culture of our birth. Immediately we began to grow in that medium, shaped and influenced by the customs, values, moral code, and social norms of our parents, community, and society. We learned the language and the laws. This growth medium is also where we learned our prejudices and our hatreds, our jealousy and our greed and our pride.

Culture Shock

Then one day we discovered the Kingdom of Heaven. We were born again and became citizens of God's Kingdom. And that's where the challenge really began. After spending 20, 30 or 40 years in a certain medium that trained us to think a certain way, we suddenly find ourselves in a whole new culture—a new growth medium—with a whole lot of new things to learn and a whole lot of old things to unlearn. And therein lies the problem: How do we get rid of the old culture in our hearts and minds to live in the new one? That's the universal challenge for every dual citizenship believer.

You see, culture is also what lies at the very center of the great cosmic conflict between the Kingdom of God and the kingdom of darkness, and earths kingdom is the battleground. The battle for earth is the battle for culture, and culture is the manifestation of the collective thinking of a people. In other words, whatever the people as a whole think collectively—their beliefs, values, ideals, etc.—becomes their culture.

So whoever controls the minds of the people controls the culture. In fact, whoever controls the minds will create the culture. The Bible says that as a man thinks in his heart, so is he (Prov. 23:7 KJV). This means that the way we think determines who we become. In this context, the heart is the mind. And the Kingdom of God is a kingdom of the heart. Therefore, the King of Heaven is battling for the minds of the creatures He created in His own image.

Culture Principles

1. Once you understand the culture of a people, you can better understand the people.
2. Culture is the act of developing the intellectual and moral faculties by education, expert care, and training.
3. Culture is the enlightenment and excellence of taste acquired by intellectual and aesthetic training.
4. Culture is the integrated pattern of human knowledge, belief, and behavior that depends upon man's capacity for learning and transmitting knowledge to succeeding generations.
5. Culture is the customary beliefs, social forms, and material traits of a racial, religious, or social group.
6. Culture is the set of shared attitudes, values, goals, and practices that characterize a company or corporation.
7. Culture means to grow in a prepared medium.

8. The battle for earth is the battle for culture

The very culture of the Kingdom is opposite of any of the cultures of this world and opposite of any common thinking of what is even accepted in earthly kingdoms. As much as we have been brainwashed by worldly mindset to think that happiness means doing whatever we want, the Kingdom of God has a culture of ethics and its own normalities. They are outlined in chapter 7 but I want to reiterate a few "Do's" that stand out to me.. We might think of these as something the Lord wants us to do not because He needs anything from us. He wants us to practice it for our own good and the health of the Kingdom you reside in:

1. When you give...
2. When you pray...
3. When you fast...

The word, WHEN denotes that this is expected. Jesus did not use "IF"...

We don't say "IF you breathe..", we say "WHEN you breathe..." because it is expected. The Kingdom of God has expectations to its citizens. (e.g. when you became American Citizens. It also means that these teachings are not optional. It's not a Preference - it's a norm.

Matthew 10:39

Whoever finds his life will lose it, and whoever loses his life for my sake will find it

Luke 6:38

> *Give, and it will be given to you. A good measure, pressed down, shaken together and running over, will be poured into your lap. For with the measure you use, it will be measured to you."*

Matthew 23:11-12

> *The greatest among you will be your servant. For those who exalt themselves will be humbled, and those who humble themselves will be exalted.*

2 Corinthians 12:9-10

> *But he said to me, "My grace is sufficient for you, for <u>my power is made perfect in weakness."</u> Therefore I will boast all the more gladly about my weaknesses, so that Christ's power may rest on me. That is why, for Christ's sake, I delight in weaknesses, in insults, in hardships, in persecutions, in difficulties. <u>For when I am weak, then I am strong.</u>*

Matthew 20: 25-28

> *Jesus called them together and said, "You know that the rulers of the Gentiles lord it over them, and their high officials exercise authority over them. 26 Not so with you. Instead, <u>whoever wants to become great among you must be your servant,</u> 27 and whoever wants to be first must be your slave— 28 just as the Son of Man did not come to be served, but to serve, and to give his life as a ransom for many."*

We see this commonly: "It shall not be so among you..."

Jesus established this as a basic principle in all three gospels.

Matthew 20:25-28

> *[25] But Jesus called them unto him, and said, Ye know that the princes of the Gentiles exercise dominion over them, and they that are great exercise authority upon them.*

> *26 <u>But it shall not be so among you:</u> but whosoever will be great among you, let him be your minister;*

> *27 And whosoever will be chief among you, let him be your servant:*

> *28 Even as the Son of man came not to be ministered unto, but to minister, and to give his life a ransom for many.*

Luke 22:26

> *26 But ye shall not be so: but he that is greatest among you, let him be as the younger; and he that is chief, as he that doth serve.*

Mark 10:43-44

> *43 But so shall it not be among you: but whosoever will be great among you, shall be your minister:*

> *44 And whosoever of you will be the chiefest, shall be servant of all.*

Although Jesus was dealing with a matter of leadership here, He also laid out the understanding for the Kingdom He leads and we live our life in the Kingdom knowing that ours is of a different culture. This is one reason we need to renew our mind daily to the Word of God, because our natural mind wants to revert to the natural Kingdom culture.. **Don't let it!**

XII

Kingdom Culmination

It is time to bring this all together for the most illustrative summary and culmination of this book so you can learn to not only understand, but know how to employ the principles and laws of the Kingdom of God in your life, and reap the true rewards of Kingdom Citizenship in every area of your existence. I want to do it by getting into the highlights and hidden nuggets of the Gospel of Mark Chapter 4, then gathering and packaging all we have learned to ignite a renewed way of thinking and living for you and your ministry as Ambassador of the Kingdom!

Jesus alludes that the understanding of this parable in Mark 4 is a key to understanding all the parables. In other words, herein lies the secret, or the mystery of the Kingdom of God, so get this understanding!

Mark is the shortest and earliest gospel. It's believed that both Matthew and Luke used the gospel of Mark as one of their sources in compiling their own gospel narratives. Many of the most famous Bible scholars view Mark as the masterpiece of all the gospels, it is because every word in the gospel of Mark was written with intentionality to weave together the story of Jesus Christ, the Son of God in such a way that by the end of the gospel everyone who's heard or read it feels compelled to fully appreciate the faith-forming skill that Mark employed in the way he told the story.

Jesus is ok with keeping his disciples in the dark in Mark's gospel, if they don't know what he meant then Jesus doesn't tend to explain his teachings to them. Also, Jesus repeatedly tells people not to tell others about the miracles and healings that he performs and instructs them not to tell others that he is the Messiah, and he silences demons that try to tell people that he is the Son of God. Jesus does not seem to want everyone to know his true identity in Mark's gospel.

Jesus didn't want his disciples to say anything about his identity as Messiah or Son of God until after his death and resurrection, for the reality of what it meant for him to be the Messiah could not be rightly interpreted apart from the cross. He was not there for glory, but for death on a cross.

The disciples are given the "secret" (closer Greek translation is Mystery) to the kingdom of God, but Jesus gets angry at his disciples for not understanding the parable

Let's get right in:

Mark 4

The Parable of the Sower

> 4 And again He began to teach by the sea. And a great multitude was gathered to Him, so that He got into a boat and sat in it on the sea; and the whole multitude was on the land facing the sea. ² Then He taught them many things by parables, and said to them in His teaching:
>
> ³ "Listen! Behold, a sower went out to sow. ⁴ And it happened, as he sowed, that some seed fell by the wayside; and the birds of the air came and devoured it. ⁵ Some fell on stony ground, where it did not have much earth; and immediately it sprang up because it had no depth of earth. ⁶ But when the sun was up it was scorched,

and because it had no root it withered away. ⁷ And some seed fell among thorns; and the thorns grew up and choked it, and it yielded no crop. ⁸ But other seed fell on good ground and yielded a crop that sprang up, increased and produced: some thirtyfold, some sixty, and some a hundred."

⁹ And He said to them, "He who has ears to hear, let him hear!"

Jesus tells the parable of the sower as explained and then says, "He who has ears to hear, let him hear!" Whenever Jesus says, "He who has ears to hear, let him hear," He is calling for people to pay careful heed. It's another way of saying, "Listen up! Pay close attention!"

The Purpose of Parables

¹⁰ But when He was alone, those around Him with the twelve asked Him about the parable. ¹¹ And He said to them, "To you it has been given to know the mystery of the kingdom of God; but to those who are outside, all things come in parables, ¹² so that

'Seeing they may see and not perceive,

And hearing they may hear and not understand;

Lest they should turn,

And their sins be forgiven them.' "

The spiritual meaning was not apparent and the twelve did not understand the parable and inquire of Jesus as to the meaning and why He speaks in parables (The Word does not specifically state that this was their question, but we can assume so by the answer Jesus gave.).

Now, I have heard many teachings on this and I have come to the personal conclusion that differs a bit from others, and maybe I am getting to granular for my own good but I wanted to share this point in its fullness of my understanding with you anyway.

The disciples, who wanted the things of God, were **given to know the mystery of the Kingdom** – they could be spoken to plainly. But others were often taught with parables. In the Bible, a mystery isn't something you can't figure out. It is something that you would not know unless God revealed it to you (Rhema). In the Biblical sense of the idea, you may know exactly what a mystery is, yet it is still a mystery because you would not have known unless God revealed it.

A parable isn't exactly an *illustration*. A good teacher can illustrate by stating a truth and then *illustrating* the truth through a story or an analogy. But when Jesus used parables, He didn't start by stating a truth. Instead, the parable was like a doorway. Jesus' listeners stood at the doorway and heard Him. If they were not interested, they stayed on the outside. But if they were interested, they could walk through the doorway and think about the truth behind the parable and what it meant to their lives.

In this case, if they really wanted to seek the Kingdom, they would find it.

Jesus states that the reason is *so that*

> *'Seeing they may see and not perceive,*
>
> *And hearing they may hear and not understand;*
>
> *Lest they should turn,*
>
> *And their sins be forgiven them.'* "

So if I break this down, He is saying that it is purposely so that I can purposely put a truth right in front of their (those outside the

12) eyes and they still will not see it so that those who dig in will get understanding and those who do not will not. I see it as a picture of grace in that if Jesus gave them a master key to the Kingdom such as this, and they willfully ignored it, they would be stuck in their sins and not forgiven, but if they do hear and understand, it is because they had an intentional revelation and thus accountable for that Word and will be forgiven of their sins. But if they didn't understand what He was saying, no accountability for this Word is held. That's how weighty the Word of God is when presented.

The Parable of the Sower Explained

> *13 And He said to them, "Do you not understand this parable? How then will you understand all the parables? 14 The sower sows the word. 15 And these are the ones by the wayside where the word is sown. When they hear, Satan comes immediately and takes away the word that was sown in their hearts. 16 These likewise are the ones sown on stony ground who, when they hear the word, immediately receive it with gladness; 17 and they have no root in themselves, and so endure only for a time. Afterward, when tribulation or persecution arises for the word's sake, immediately they stumble. 18 Now these are the ones sown among thorns; they are the ones who hear the word, 19 and the cares of this world, the deceitfulness of riches, and the desires for other things entering in choke the word, and it becomes unfruitful. 20 But these are the ones sown on good ground, those who hear the word, accept it, and bear fruit: some thirtyfold, some sixty, and some a hundred."*

Jesus seemingly gets a little annoyed with them and asks [My paraphrase] "Don't you understand this? C'mon guys, how will you understand anything else if you can't get this?"

In the parable above, the sower sows the word. The seed being sown is actually the "Word" from the Greek root word *logos*. The definition of *logos* is written words, speaking, instruction, decrees and reason. In John 1 however, we read: In the beginning was the Word, and the Word was with God, and the Word was God... Jesus is the Word. Jesus, the King is synonymous with Gods Word, He is truth. The sower sowing the word is anyone sowing or teaching the Gospel of Jesus (Luke 8:11), and by extension, the sower himself, is one who spreads or expands the Kingdom of God.

As with all the examples of the soil, it is possible for Gods truth to take root in one area, but not others. We can have a revelation of one area of the Kingdom and even display its fruit in our lives, but other areas are still dry, awaiting revealed truth.

The word that is sown by the wayside is on the hard path of the side of the road where gravel and garbage lay. Verse 15 interprets the birds in chapter 4 as being Satan. We know according to John 10:10 that the thief (Satan) comes to steal kill and destroy; and that is his ploy here. But its not the enemies fault the seed, or the revelation was stolen; he did what he was supposed to do... steal; The sower did his job, so that leaves the ground to be the cause of issue.

So we have the four types of ground or hearts that the Word gets sown into: wayside Ground, Stony Ground, Thorny Ground and finally, good ground. Since this is not an exhaustive teaching of Mark 4 and the seed, I will not get into each individual sowing, but to say that with respect to the Gospel of the Kingdom, it is clear that it is always the responsibility of the hearer to understand, always.

Jesus tells them that unto them it is given to know the mystery of the Kingdom. Remember, Jesus is the Word... Jesus is the King, the Gospel of the King is the Gospel of the Kingdom, which is what Jesus is illuminating here... He wants them (you) to enter into the Kingdom whereby this revelation of all your constitutional (biblical) rights, privileges, benefits and authority to have dominion are not only unlocked, and available, but bestowed upon you just for being a part of it and understanding your citizenship.

Light Under a Basket

> *²¹ Also He said to them, "Is a lamp brought to be put under a basket or under a bed? Is it not to be set on a lampstand? ²² For there is nothing hidden which will not be revealed, nor has anything been kept secret but that it should come to light. ²³ If anyone has ears to hear, let him hear."*

> *²⁴ Then He said to them, "Take heed what you hear. With the same measure you use, it will be measured to you; and to you who hear, more will be given. ²⁵ For whoever has, to him more will be given; but whoever does not have, even what he has will be taken away from him."*

[My paraphrase]

Everything I am telling you about the Kingdom and the power will come to light because eventually all that is hidden will be revealed (Rev 11:15)... if you can understand this listen close.

Be very careful of what you listen to, because the world will feed you garbage to pollute and dilute this; but if you fully understand it, you will grow in the power and authority of the kingdom; in fact, with the measure of your understanding, is the measure that you will thrive within the Kingdom principles. And if you have no understanding, you will not see the Kingdom at all.

The Parable of the Growing Seed

> *²⁶ And He said, "The kingdom of God is as if a man should scatter seed on the ground, ²⁷ and should sleep by night and rise by day, and the seed should sprout and grow, he himself does not*

know how. ²⁸ For the earth yields crops by itself: first the blade, then the head, after that the full grain in the head. ²⁹ But when the grain ripens, immediately he puts in the sickle, because the harvest has come."

This is pretty literal in its application because He directly correlates it to the Kingdom: *The kingdom of God is as if a man should scatter seed on the ground, and should sleep by night and rise by day, and the seed should sprout and grow, he himself does not know how. For the earth yields crops by itself: first the blade, then the head, after that the full grain in the head.*

This is how the Kingdom works when you understand it.. You do not work it or try to make things happen, your rights are automatic once you have an understanding of the principle of the Kingdom.

But when the grain ripens, immediately he puts in the sickle, because the harvest has come."

Jesus said in Mathew 24:14 that the Gospel of the Kingdom will be preached throughout the earth so that all the nations will hear it, then the end will come.. This verse seems to echo that sentiment in that the Kingdom is not yet spread throughout the earth, but once it is, we will see the full manifestation of the corn in the ear, or the grain in the head.. or better... the Glory of the Lord will cover the earth as the oceans cover the sea.

The Parable of the Mustard Seed

³⁰ Then He said, "To what shall we liken the kingdom of God? Or with what parable shall we picture it? ³¹ It is like a mustard seed which, when it is sown on the ground, is smaller than all the seeds on earth; ³² but when it is sown, it grows up and becomes greater than all herbs, and shoots out large branches, so that the birds of the air may nest under its shade."

Another parable to drive this home! Let's liken the Kingdom of God to a tiny mustard seed (one man Adam with a mandate that was later resurrected with Christ), that when it was planted it was small, but when it is culminated it will be in its full Glory!

Jesus' Use of Parables

> *33 And with many such parables He spoke the word to them as they were able to hear it.*

> *34 But without a parable He did not speak to them. And when they were alone, He explained all things to His disciples.*

Recapitulation and an inference of other parables were told to them and further explained, that are not written. Jesus must have really wanted to drive this home and get this into their understanding!

After all that teaching about the Kingdom, Jesus wanted to then put His Words to the test to see if they caught the revelation and said "Let us cross over to the other side".. Remember, He was already in the boat teaching, they were on the dry land.... One of the Gospels says that He constrained them to get in the boat. He is about to see if they understand the Kingdom authority they've just been soaking in the knowledge of all day... Let's see...

Wind and Wave Obey Jesus

> *35 On the same day, when evening had come, He said to them, "Let us cross over to the other side." 36 Now when they had left the multitude, they took Him along in the boat as He was. And other little boats were also with Him. 37 And a great windstorm arose, and the waves beat into the boat, so that it was already filling. 38 But He was in the stern, asleep on a pillow. And they awoke Him and said to Him, "Teacher, do You not care that we are perishing?"*

³⁹ Then He arose and rebuked the wind, and said to the sea, "Peace, be still!" And the wind ceased and there was a great calm. ⁴⁰ But He said to them, "Why are you so fearful? How is it that you have no faith?" ⁴¹ And they feared exceedingly, and said to one another, "Who can this be, that even the wind and the sea obey Him!"

Jesus takes advantage of the time to catch a nap after teaching all day (preaching that long will tire anyone!). and the account states that a great windstorm arose, and the waves beat into the boat, so that it was filling up... And where was the King Jesus? Asleep on a pillow in the back of the boat!

The twelve had their chance right here to prove their understanding and exercise their authority; everything they knew and thought they knew was being put to the test, and what did they do? They ran to Him, woke him up and asked Him to do something!

> *Then He arose and rebuked the wind, and said to the sea, "Peace, be still!" And the wind ceased and there was a great calm*

Here Jesus is exercising the same authority of the Kingdom that they have and that you and I have.. At the very least, they should have trusted that if Jesus was in the boat it wouldn't sink! But they missed their opportunity.

> *But He said to them, "Why are you so fearful? How is it that you have no faith?" ⁴¹ And they feared exceedingly, and said to one another, "Who can this be, that even the wind and the sea obey Him!"*

Jesus' frustration had grown from the beginning because now He just spent all day teaching them about the Kingdom. He sown the Word in to their hearts and all they did was prove that it was wayside ground by allowing the enemy to steal it with fear only less than an hour later!

I am certain Jesus' voice was loud when He asked *"Why are you so fearful? How is it that you have no faith?"* And rather than understand at this point, the bible tells us that then *"..they feared exceedingly, and said to one another, "Who can this be, that even the wind and the sea obey Him!"*

Then they came to the other side of the sea, to the country of the Gadarenes, and immediately there was a man with an unclean spirit. When he saw Jesus from afar, he ran and worshiped Him.

> *⁷ And he cried out with a loud voice and said, "What have I to do with You, Jesus, Son of the Most High God? I implore[c] You by God that You do not torment me." ⁸ For He said to him, "Come out of the man, unclean spirit!"*

Jesus healed the man by casting the demons into the pigs who then ran off the cliff and drowned in the water. Jesus invoked this Kingdom authority once again and then told the healed man to tell everyone of what happened. (subdue and multiply). Everywhere Jesus went, He preached the Kingdom and demonstrated it.

1 Thessalonians 1:5

> *For our gospel [of the Kingdom] came not unto you in word only, but also in power, and in the Holy Ghost,*

When this Gospel of the Kingdom is preached, there should be a demonstration of power with it; because **you cannot have Kingdom without Power, and you cannot have power without Glory.**

Are ready to be live and operate in a way and on level that people cannot understand how you get the results that you get in life? Then lets grab the Keys and put all this together for use!

XIII

Take the Keys

The keys to the Kingdom of God should allow you to work and live in a level that blow peoples minds...

You can and should be living and operating in a way that people in the world cannot understand how you get the results that you get in life.

When Jesus came to earth to restore and extend the Kingdom of God, some who acknowledged Him as King thought the Kingdom would come through revolution. They thought there would be an actual physical revolt against the existing ruling powers of the world. But Jesus taught that the key to His Kingdom was not revolution but one of repentance (Changing the way you used to think and think the King-dom way)

Mathew 16

> *¹³ When Jesus came into the coasts of Caesarea Philippi, he asked his disciples, saying, Whom do men say that I the Son of man am?*
>
> *¹⁴ And they said, Some say that thou art John the Baptist: some, Elias; and others, Jeremias, or one of the prophets.*
>
> *¹⁵ He saith unto them, But whom say ye that I am?*

16 And Simon Peter answered and said, Thou art the Christ, the Son of the living God.

17 And Jesus answered and said unto him, Blessed art thou, Simon Barjona: for flesh and blood hath not revealed it unto thee, but my Father which is in heaven.

18 And I say also unto thee, That thou art Peter, and upon this rock I will build my church; and the gates of hell shall not prevail against it.

19 And I will give unto thee the keys of the kingdom of heaven: and whatsoever thou shalt bind on earth shall be bound in heaven: and whatsoever thou shalt loose on earth shall be loosed in heaven.

As citizens of the Kingdom of God, we should never need to depend on man to heal our people or provide for our needs. That responsibility is our King's responsibility.

He is the one who created and saved us; God is the one who brought us into the Kingdom, under His rule, in His domain, so we are His responsibility. Some say that the Lord God heals us through the physician's hands and skills. But my question to that is, does the Lord God need assistance from any man to heal? He is God all by Himself. He created us! All that the Lord God requires from you is to put all of your faith in Him.

Before Jesus returned to Heaven He told His disciples:

Luke 22:29

And I appoint unto you a Kingdom, as my Father hath appointed unto me.

Jesus also spoke of His government of the Kingdom (Church) which would extend the message of the Kingdom throughout the world:

Matthew 16:18-19

> *And I say also unto thee, That thou art Peter, and upon this rock I will build my church; and the gates of Hell shall not prevail against it. And I will give unto thee the keys of the Kingdom of Heaven: and whatsoever thou shalt bind on earth shall be bound in Heaven; and whatsoever thou shalt loose on earth shall be loosed in Heaven.*

Keys are systems, principles of laws within the kingdom of God... Precepts and principles to make certain things within the Kingdom open up and happen. The purpose of these keys is to fulfill the mandate of *Thy Kingdom Come*. In other words, Jesus said to pray that Gods Kingdom comes on earth as it is in heaven... He later gave us the keys so that we can perform it as Ambassadors and whatsoever we bind on earth shall be bound in Heaven; and whatsoever we loose on earth shall be loosed in Heaven.. The kingdom is restored, justice prevailed and the keys are yours as a citizen of the Kingdom!

Jesus gave us the Keys, that's plural.. not a singular key, but keys. And note that there's a difference between keys TO the Kingdom and keys *of* the Kingdom. Jesus said he gives us the keys OF the kingdom. Here is the difference between ignorance and knowledge...The key TO the Kingdom is imputed righteousness; the keys OF the Kingdom are its ways of operation.

If someone gives me a full set of keys... I may be uncertain as to what they all go to although I have the power in my hands to enter houses drive cars, sail boats, bank accounts and many other things that these keys unlock, but my ignorance is preventing me from obtaining it, knowledge is the key to the keys! What I have given you in this book is the knowledge to access and to use the keys.

The holder of the keys holds the power.

Understand the that Kingdom is one of perfect order, it is your task to ensure that everything is in order.. if there is a spirit in the way of your expanding the kingdom, you have the authority to cast it out, and it must obey because you are operating in the highest level of authority and order. If someone is sick in your presence, heal them, deliver them because it is a violation of Kingdom law for you to operate under the Kingdom rule and governance and for these to exist. There is no sickness in the Kingdom, you have the authority to change that and remove the sickness.

Paul is arrested and on a ship headed to Italy when the seas were contrary and Paul (no doubt to lessen the mens fears) admonishes them to eat and tells them that everyone will live, but the boat will not make it (because he was plugged into the Kingdom and heard it from the Governor).. The next day the ship struck a sandbar and ran aground. The bow stuck fast and the stern was broken into pieces by the pounding of the surf. They were all shipwrecked on the island of Malta and built a fire because it was raining and cold. Paul gathered a pile of brushwood and put it on the fire. The heat drove a poisonous snake out of the brushwood and the snake fastened itself on Paul's hand. The islanders saw the snake hanging from his hand. They said to each other, "This man must be a murderer. He escaped from the sea, but justice won't allow him to live." <u>Paul shook the snake off into the fire and suffered no ill effects</u>. When nothing happened to Paul, the islanders changed their minds and said Paul was a god.

Because He was a citizen of the Kingdom, even nature responded differently!

Paul had the keys and knew how to use them... Check out (Acts 16:16-40), Paul and Silas were accused of crimes by slave-owners whose income they had indirectly interfered with by invoking the Kingdom upon and freeing a fortune-telling slave girl from demon possession. These owners stirred up a lynch mob, resulting in Paul and Silas being severely beaten at the direction of the mob-accommodating city leaders, and subsequently consigned in shackles to the city jail. Paul's message to them: "We are Roman citizens, and you have beaten us and jailed us without cause." The magistrates were fear struck upon learning that they had violated the sacred civil rights of two Roman citizens, an action which could have subjected the rulers to severe personal penalties, perhaps up to and including execution. Profuse apologies followed, and a request that the abused men quietly leave the city.

... That's the same as us and the kingdom of God, we can pull that same card!

Citizenship empowers an individual; citizenship provides legitimate access to all the rights and privileges of a constitution and a country. Becoming a citizen, especially a citizen of a kingdom such as the Kingdom of God, means that you become powerful. Your citizenship is the source of your personal authority where those rights are concerned. You have the power to demand things. By the power of your citizenship, you can call in constitutional privileges and promises. The constitution is more powerful than the citizens, just as the law is more powerful than the lawyer or the judge that exercises it and certainly more powerful than the politicians who talk about it. Good citizens have access to the full protection and advantage of the law.

A key to the Kingdom of God is understanding the government, the way the government works within the Kingdom, and your access to it

Jesus said I gave you the keys to the Kingdom... You have the keys to the whole kingdom... So you should not be sitting around waiting for a miracle when you have the keys. You should not be waiting on God for something to come your way because you have the keys... Don't be begging God for your healing when you have the key... Don't you dare

beg for what you already own: you have the keys to heaven and earth...
YOU HAVE DOMINION Make it happen... Speak it into existence,
speak the language of the kingdom, go into the kingdom and open up
the doors down to earth.

A key is access.. you have the access to everything in the Kingdom!
Do you get this? A key also represents ownership and the authority
of management over it by the owner, so do not think that the enemy
has any right to come into your house, where you hold the keys and
take anything. He would be stealing from the King, from God Himself
because the earth is the Lords and the fullness thereof...

Remember what we said earlier that in a kingdom, everything belongs
to the king, even the subjects, or the people... It comes down to culture
again because we do not understand the completeness of Lordship because the only Lord we recognize in America is our Landlord... But it's
the same premise the landlord of the world, you live there, get it? Earth
is the Lords. So in the kingdom there is no ownership, it is all the Lords,
but you have the keys and access to it all.

That's why in the kingdom there is no real prosperity teaching because
it is a commonwealth, everybody is wealthy there... Everybody has access
to everything. This is why when we seek the Kingdom first and His
righteousness ALL these things are added to us.. because it's a commonwealth and you have full right to it all!

Jesus separates the politics when they ask him if he pays taxes, and he
said *"show me a coin, ...who's image is on it?"*

That must be Caesars...

Matthew 22:21

> *They say unto him, Caesar's. Then saith he unto them, Render therefore unto Caesar the things which are Caesar's; and unto God the things that are God's.*

What He saying is Caesar has his government, and I have mine, whatever has his image on it must be his... **But those who have my image (us as citizens of the Kingdom) on them, must be mine!**

Here's a problem with the church... We preach the gospel of Jesus Christ, but we don't preach the gospel that Jesus preached... I know that sounds harsh but Jesus didn't say to preach prosperity: and although the Kingdom benefits are so much more, Jesus didn't even say to preach how to be happy and 99 ways to be blessed...

Jesus preached the Kingdom, the disciples preached the Kingdom, Paul also preached the Kingdom then preached Christ... and everywhere the Kingdom was preached, signs and wonders followed because the Kingdom was made manifest.

Acts 20:25

> *And indeed, now I know that you all, among whom I have gone preaching the kingdom of God, will see my face no more.*

Within the midst of his final address, he made this statement as a summary of his teaching in Ephesus. This is significant because it shows us that Paul's message perfectly synchronized with the teachings of Jesus Christ. Throughout His ministry, Jesus Christ taught and emphasized the Kingdom of God as the core of His message (Matthew 4:17, 23; Mark 1:15; John 18:36).

Jesus said as you go preach this Kingdom

And as ye go, preach, saying, The kingdom of heaven is at hand.

1 Corinthians 4:20 says: the *Kingdom of God is not in word but in in power...*

1 Thessalonians 1:5 Paul says

> *"For our gospel came not unto you in word only, but also in power, and in the Holy Ghost, and in much assurance; as ye know what manner of men we were among you for your sake. "*

... Our gospel is not only word but power

Matthew 24:14

> *And this gospel of the kingdom shall be preached in all the world for a witness unto all nations; and then shall the end come.*

Why don't we see the power in the church today? No one is preaching it!!!!

YOU are a citizen of the Kingdom Jesus and the foundational Apostles preached. **You are sanctioned with the keys to reveal the Kingdom the Power and the Glory** and to go forth and advance the Kingdom mandate by living a life that represents the Kingdom and bestowing the Kingdom culture every place you go and every place your feet tread.

He gave you the Power!

Luke 10:19

> *Behold, I give unto you power to tread on serpents and scorpions, and over all the power of the enemy: and nothing shall by any means hurt you.*

It is not enough to believe Jesus can do it. It is not enough to believe God for something in your life, you need to start realizing the power and authority you have because not only can God do it, not only can Jesus do it, but you can also because the same spirit that raised Christ from the dead also dwells in you (Romans 8:11), and the King Himself has authorized you to have dominion over every situation!

OK, I am preaching now! Remember the disciples on the water in a great storm? It was Mathew 14.. The bible says Jesus forced (constrained) the disciples to get in the boat.. He knew there was a storm brewing and He pushed them into it! The account states that the waves and the wind were contrary to them and in the middle of their trial, here comes Jesus walking on the water! The disciples were scared and thought it was a ghost, but Peter says, Lord, if it is you, bid me to come out. What was He saying? Authorize me! Now get this..... Jesus authorized Peter to step out of the problem and walk on top of the very thing that was coming against them and trying to kill him. Jesus authorized him and he did it!

Jesus authorized them to walk on top of every situation.

Mathew 10:1

> And when he had called unto him his twelve disciples, he gave them power against unclean spirits, to cast them out, and to heal all manner of sickness and all manner of disease.

King Jesus authorized you to walk on top of every situation.

How much have you missed out on in life because you did not believe that you were righteous enough and/or had the authority or the ability to do it? **The time is now to step into your Kingdom authority without limits!**

Learn to use your power and authority and evict the enemy every place he has a foothold. Seek the Kingdom first and stop worrying about the wars and rumors of wars; stop worrying about the economy, inflation and what's disappearing on the shelves. You are a Kingdom citizen so not using your power and authority through the given keys are limiting the King who provided them to you; and then many question why God didn't do something, but it wasn't Him who didn't do it, it was you.

You can either beg God to do something for you, or you can enforce the law and make it happen!

Can you imagine a government that does not know how to take care of its own?

Can you imagine how the Roman senate was taken care of during a time of war and how they were protected?

When there was a famine in Egypt, there was bread in every house where the mark of the Lord was...

Do you get that?

But what you need to fully understand is that money isn't your source, and that you don't always need a bakery to get bread. The kingdom has 101 ways to get to you what you need that you aren't even aware of... Stop being so close minded and think that the world, or that the kingdom of this world needs to provide for you.

The Bible never tells you where the bread comes from in the house of Israel when there was famine... and I don't care if I don't know, all I need to know, is that the Kingdom provides it because the King loves me and because I am a citizen of His.

The pursuit of worldly power is simply the misplaced pursuit of mans lost dominion...The world seeks it aimlessly and is never filled because

it is the wrong power they pursue. Jesus our King restored your dominion and gave you power and authorized you to use it. Atop of that He
pardoned every past, present and future offence off your account and
placed you, and made you spotless before the Throne so no man (not
even you) can ever accuse you of a crime again.

My prayer for you right now is that as you go about your life being
in this world, but not of it, that you represent the Kingdom of God
in all you do, and that you be an effective witness to the Goodness of
the King.

Show people how to gain entry, heal them, deliver them, set them free
and show them the attributes and culture of our Kingdom so they will
know that what you speak of is real.

And finally, May the King commend you for your service when its
time is over and may you hear: *"Well done, good and faithful servant!
You have been faithful with a few things; I will put you in charge of
many things. Come and share your master's happiness!"* (Matt. 25:21,
NIV)—those are the words I hope you will hear when you reach your
home country, The Kingdom of Heaven.

I had a dream in 2019 right before the COVID pandemic where the Lord showed me things to come in the coming years. This was concerning the church, His Ecclesia. Things have been unfolding exactly as He showed me and I know there is much more to come that we need to be ready for. The dream was not to scare me, but to prepare me and to put me on course to search out His kingdom in a deeper way than ever before for the purpose of equipping those who will press into the Kingdom.

The year is 2022. It is no secret that we are in unprecedented times and that the last days are near, and upon us. Even the world sees it unfolding before their eyes. Truth be told, I am so excited to see all this unfolding before me because that means God chose me (and you) to be born right now, in this day and age, for a specific reason and purpose.

King Jesus said these things not only will happen, but must happen (Mathew 24). But as you now know with certainty, the King looks out for His own.

Matthew 6:33

> *But seek ye first the kingdom of God, and his righteousness; and all these things shall be added unto you.*

Take this to heart. Jesus said that after the other things the gentiles seek, but you must seek the Kingdom first, with and in His righteousness, and all provision will be made open to you.

And while people will inevitably suffer and live with fear, lack, sickness, etc... they will look upon you at the peace and sustenance you have and ask why are you not suffering as we? Then you explain everything about your King and His Kingdom.

Mathew 24:

> *⁷ For nation shall rise against nation, and kingdom against king-dom: and there shall be famines, and pestilences, and earthquakes, in divers places.*
>
> *¹⁴ And this gospel of the kingdom shall be preached in all the world for a witness unto all nations; and then shall the end come.*

OK, Finally my brethren! Commune with the King! Speaking the language of the Kingdom as much and as often as possible will allow the King to impart His Wisdom and knowledge into your spirit for every situation in your life. This is paramount.

Some information in this book was taken from various teachings of the Late Dr. Myles Monroe, to whom I will thank when we meet in the Kingdom of Heaven;

Art Thomas Blog, The King James Bible and other forms as noted

About The Author

Anthony Reinglas was initially ordained through Covenant Ministries International by the late, David T. Demola of Faith Fellowship Ministries, and is founder and President of Xtreme Church (Xtreme1038), an apostolic ministry focused on building the Kingdom of God and end time revival. Through Xtreme Church Anthony and His lovely wife Lisa have pioneered several other ministries. Anthony is currently Vice President of the Board at SonRise Faith Church (where his mother is Pastor). He and Lisa are also the Apostolic founders of CrossRoads Worship Center of NJ, Celebrate Hope Recovery Center in Staten Island NY and several other local ministries as well as the national Gods4Me ministry which reaches people all over the USA with electronic media, billboards and more.

Anthony's' teachings can be found online at most of his websites listed below.

In addition to the above, Anthony Reinglas councils with other Pastors and leaders assisting them in growing their ministries to their fullest potential in the Kingdom and performs public speaking appearances.

"My heart's desire is only to see the fullness of Kingdom of God in all its Glory, here on earth".

XtremeChurch.org
ElijahAnointing.com

IMissedTheRapture.com

Gods4Me.com
CelebrateHopeNYC.com

9 798986 187105